THE
NIGEL LAWSON
DIET
COOKBOOK

Thérèse Lawson

THE
NIGEL LAWSON
DIET
COOKBOOK

HEADLINE

First published in 1998 by HEADLINE BOOK PUBLISHING

10 9 8 7 6 5 4 3 2 1

British Library Cataloguing in Publication Data
Lawson, Thérèse
    The Nigel Lawson diet Cookbook
    1. Reducing diets – Recipes
    I.   Title
    641.5'635

ISBN 0 7472 2233 9

Home economist: Kathryn Hawkins
Stylist: Helen Trent
Designer: Peter Ward

Typeset by Letterpart Ltd, Reigate, Surrey
Printed and bound in Great Britain by
Butler & Tanner Ltd, Frome and London

HEADLINE BOOK PUBLISHING
A division of Hodder Headline PLC
338 Euston Road
London NW1 3BH

Acknowledgements

Book writing must frequently be a family affair if only because of the preoccupation of the author at home. Even more so with a book on food. My first thanks go to all my family for their patient understanding and for sampling my efforts, sometimes repetitively: they will not forget jelly week. Nor will I.

Jacqui Etheridge typed and tested the recipes and has been tireless and encouraging at all times. Her family too know the recipes off by heart. Enca San Miguel and Veronica Mavor also helped with recipes that I was nervous about. Julie Savery has continued to run the household magnificently, against quite some odds in terms of dirty saucepans.

All my wonderful friends seem to have excused my short temper and I am particularly grateful to Samuel Brittan for giving me a desk and much else for the execution of this enterprise.

I am indebted to Sainsbury's *The Magazine* for showing faith and giving me my first job in cookery writing. Heather Holden-Brown, my publisher, feels like a friend and I hope will stay one. She couldn't have been a more sensitive support.

The publisher would like to thank the following photographers and agencies for their kind permission to reproduce the photographs in this book:
Page 17 Empics; 23 Jonathan Pilkington; 71 *Times* Newspapers; 81 Herbie Knott/The *Independent*; 138 Rex Features.

While every effort has been made by the author and the publishers to trace copyright holders of photographs, in some cases this has not been possible. They apologise to those whose names may have been inadvertently missed.

For the family

Contents

Notes

Recipes suitable for vegetarians are marked with a V symbol.

Recipes have been tested with a fan-assisted electric oven, an Aga cooker and a 650-watt microwave oven, where relevant.

Imperial and metric measures appear in all recipes. Use only one set of measures and not a mixture of the two.

Some of the recipes in this book contain lightly-cooked eggs. People vulnerable to health risks, such as pregnant and nursing mothers, elderly people, invalids, babies and young children, might wish to avoid these dishes.

Introduction

This book is a compilation of recipes and tricks that I have used over the last three years and more to ensure that Nigel, my husband, would not put back the excess weight he lost on his diet. For details, see *The Nigel Lawson Diet Book*, Penguin Books, 1997. Not a tall man, he had reached almost 17 stone. He needed to lose 5 stone to become a healthy size and he did, in the space of a year.

Nigel did not want to be bothered with counting calories. This was after his Chancellorship and he had more than likely had enough of counting. Luckily, calorie knowledge is embedded in my subconscious, as with so many women of my generation.

By far the most pleasing aspect is that his weight loss has been maintained for long enough to deduce that the new slim shape is permanent and that the method works. Nigel has eaten, frequently in most cases, every single recipe I have given – and a lot more.

So, that is the subject of this book: how to maintain your weight loss while eating well, healthily, happily and forever after. I very much hope that the tricks and ideas that appear over and over in the recipes are clear and I am sure that they are adaptable to whatever foods appeal to a particular palate. In fact I devised a diet for one friend who can't abide vegetables: he has shed 2½ stone in a year, and will soon be on this maintenance plan.

Successful diets need to be tailor-made. This is a crucial point: if you can continue to enjoy most of your favourite tastes and dishes, even if played about with a bit to reduce the excesses, the likelihood of keeping up the pattern is greater because you don't feel punished. A good example is the sauce I concocted to substitute for hollandaise and mayonnaise, favourites in our household. *Lemon Sauce* (see recipe on page 131) contains only eggs, stock and lemon and is nearly as good as hollandaise. Similarly, I now make soufflés with lower-fat cheese, less butter, and skimmed milk: they remain puffy and delicious.

Remember that it is the cumulative effect of your efforts that counts. Each step is tiny in itself but really does add up (or, more accurately, subtract). Furthermore, with this approach you don't notice any frightening change or get cravings, and I am sure it is true that your body adapts to what is in fact a healthier diet and feels and functions better. Certainly Nigel says he feels very fit and indeed he can do many more things of a physical nature now than when he was fat.

A happy corollary to this approach is that the occasional sinful breakout is hardly a tragedy. If a fabulously rich chocolate pudding created by a master chef comes your way, don't reject it if you feel like it. Enjoy it. The point is to keep, automatically and on the whole, to your new habits and pattern. (Somewhat indelicately, I will tell you that once you've got all this under your belt, your system will rebel if you go berserk and you will want to break out only now and again.)

Adopt a quality rather than a quantity threshold. There are times when it is not appropriate to display fussiness, and when I think of the starving people of the world, I wonder how we who are so over-fed dare to pontificate, but I will spoil this whole enterprise if I give vent to my worries at this point. If circumstances force you to accept food that is really not nice or cooked in loads of grease, or warmed up à point for salmonella, just eat as little as you can get away with. I've noticed that when one feels hungry, a little something rapidly gets rid of the hollow feeling. If one stopped there and didn't proceed to fill up as if there were never going to be anything more to eat, a lot of excess weight would disappear.

It is the same with the finishing-up syndrome, particularly common with just-post-war people like me. We really were very hungry then and there simply wasn't enough to eat. You didn't contemplate leaving anything on the plate, and we automatically ate the most prized things first. To this day, I cannot help going first for the meat or fish, then the green vegetables, and finally the Yorkshire pudding and potatoes. For quite different reasons, this sequence is useful for modern dieters. And don't pile food on your plate or your subconscious guilt will make you finish it. Get used to taking smaller portions.

The next important factor to grasp is the idea of what 'fattening' really means. Everybody needs a certain regular amount of nourishing food to survive and function well, although this amount will vary from one person to the next. So you start off with a pretty generous credit balance in what you can eat. If you regularly eat more than this amount, you will gain weight – eat less and you will lose weight.

The crucial way to reduce your intake is consciously to adapt your cooking *methods*. A lot of excess weight is accounted for by what we add to basic food when we cook with fats, add sauces, sweeten, thicken or serve with a knob of butter. Utensils can help here: non-stick frying pans are a tremendous asset for dieters as you can cook in the minimum of oil or even none. For the same reason, steaming, poaching and microwaving are great cooking methods. Grilling too, of course. And wonderful results can be achieved by roasting or casseroling without using fat or lots of flour. Cooking foods in parcels of paper or foil in the oven keeps the contents moist, concentrates the flavours, and requires little or no fat (for example, see *Trout Baked in a Parcel* on page 80). Allowing meaty casseroles to go cold after cooking enables you to skim off easily any fat that's been produced during the cooking process, either with a sieve spoon or by lifting it off with kitchen paper. Such dishes often improve when reheated: the flavours become even more concentrated second time around. Many of my recipes incorporate the principle of 'self-thickening sauces', which simply means mushing some of the ingredients in the dish to achieve an appetising, thick consistency at the end (for example, see *Boozy Pork with Apple* on page 110).

In general, the better the quality of the food you are cooking the less embellishment it needs, and it is the embellishments that quite often cause the problem of overweight. If you have beautifully fresh and carefully prepared vegetables, their flavour is such that the addition of butter, which can be somewhat of a habit, is quite unnecessary. Interestingly, a squeeze of fresh lemon juice instead can enhance some green vegetables in a delightful way. A beautifully grilled Dover sole is wonderful, perhaps even at its best, served simply with lemon wedges: you don't need butter sauce. The difficulty is that such prime foods are, generally, very expensive. You could take the view that you prefer to pay more for the quality whenever you can and, as recompense, be prepared to eat humble, but nevertheless delicious and nutritious food, more often than you are used to. Sunday's beef doesn't have to be sirloin: pot-roasted brisket is also a treat and tremendous value for money (for example, see *Hot Pot Beef* on page 105). Many dishes based on vegetables are not only very satisfying and tasty but far more economical too (for example, see *Broccoli and Cauliflower Mustard-Cheese* on page 60).

Another budget-balancing device, if you like really good food and also like to cook, is to eat out less and instead have serious treats at home: it can cost a fraction of even an indifferent meal out. We tend to do this for birthdays and anniversaries, and go for bust (see recipe for *Buckwheat Blinis* and accompaniments on page 33). Not that I mean to be a killjoy: I'm the first to say 'yes' to a proposal to go out for a meal, I love it, and I do not wish to imply that anyone should feel guilty for sometimes hating their own kitchen and abandoning it. Or buying in a ready-made meal or take-away, come to that. Be careful with ready-mades, though. Often, the only reason for them counting as slimmers' versions is that they come in smaller quantities. Occasionally they are loaded with cream to produce an allegedly exotic sauce.

One of the reasons I frequently specify specially-flavoured oils (circumspectly, of course), certain kinds of alcohol, flavourings, spices and herbs in my recipes is that food that is well-flavoured reduces the need to smother with sauce, add mayonnaise, swamp in gravy, add butter, and a range of other fattening habits. It is a ploy to bear in mind.

The principles to apply in cooking for weight maintenance that I have alluded to are immensely simple and obvious, and once I'd embarked on this lark, it soon became second nature to me to incorporate them in my shopping and cooking. The profusion of lower-fat products is of great help, and I make liberal use of every such aid I come across. Silly though I may look, I am now in the habit of taking my reading glasses to the shops, so that I can scrutinise the nutritional information. (If manufacturers printed it in a decent size, I wouldn't have to put on my spectacles.) You need to do this: some of the claims around are spurious and annoyingly misleading. Bear in mind, for example, that 'lower fat' only means lower, possibly by an infinitesimal amount, than the original fattening product. '98% fat free' may be true, but check the sugar content carefully. Another reason for reading the information is that you may have strong views about how much artificial substance you are prepared to admit into your diet or that of your children. Sometimes the cost, in these terms, of a less-fattening version of a product is too high, and you will want to decide to buy instead the less adulterated, if more calorific, version.

Of course there are times and recipes when proper butter or good olive oil, say, are essential for the taste. If you are not prepared to be flexible on such occasions, it may be better not to cook those dishes at all. What is surprising though, once you're in the swing of it, is how frequently the lower-fat or reduced sugar version works perfectly well, sometimes even better. Throughout the recipes in this book, I have specified products that illustrate this principle.

Genuine originality in cooking is rare indeed and a marvel to sample. One of the perks of our time living in Downing Street (which was largely nightmarish for me – it is not a role one is trained for and the constant, intense scrutiny of one's inadequate self aired in public is deeply discomforting) was undoubtedly the banquets we attended. I must say that the Buckingham Palace and Windsor Castle food impressed me profoundly, not least because of the sheer perfection of the presentation. Well, naturally, I suppose. There is little I enjoy more than experiencing the products of a brilliant, professional chef. I often try to reproduce simpler versions at home, sometimes successfully and often not.

Although all the recipes in this book are my own, in the sense that I have concocted, cooked and written them, I am sure that there must be ideas, tastes and techniques of other people's that I have soaked up over the years: I am of the type that reads cookery books in bed and copies ideas from menus.

But I think some recipe books fall into the trap of being too complicated, with long and obscure ingredients lists and fancy manoeuvres. Complicated recipes at home don't necessarily work out, which can be rather dispiriting. I'm not sure it is even appropriate: at home you want to cook lovely homely things. Possibly the key to being considered a good cook is to cook precisely what people want to eat at your place: it is no coincidence that children tend to think that their own mother (forgive the politically-incorrect innuendo) is the best cook in the world.

My recipes are not intended to imitate restaurant food – that would be a lost cause in any case. They are intended to be simple, practical, reasonably economical overall, healthy, and, I very much hope, delicious: above all to demonstrate that you can eat well and imaginatively and still stay slim.

Ingredients

To save boring repetition in every recipe, here are recommendations for ingredients that I use regularly and which you might like to stock up with:

SALT use finely ground sea salt
PEPPER use black peppercorns, or a mixture of black and white, freshly ground at the time
FLOUR use plain, organic white
BUTTER use unsalted, preferably from Normandy
MILK use semi-skimmed
EGGS use large, free-range
PARMESAN use parmigiano reggiano which is the best and authentic. Avoid tubs of ready-grated Parmesan, which tastes musty

OILS use the best quality available of the specified variety in every case

FRUIT AND VEGETABLE JUICES use the unsweetened varieties

LEMONS AND OTHER FRUIT unless using just for their juice, be sure to buy unwaxed fruit

GELATINE the most widely available product is gelatine powder or granules sold in conveniently sized packs that set a pint of liquid. Leaf gelatine is, however, more fun

Nigel has always shopped reluctantly but enjoys the results – rather too much in the past, as can be observed in this photograph of him and Emily

to use. You can also get a vegetarian product that certainly works but tends to produce a slightly rubbery result – it contains gum. However, if concerned about BSE-related problems, this is a useful alternative. There is also agar-agar, a setting agent made from seaweed, which sounds more appealing but is harder to obtain. The choice is yours.

If you find gelatine difficult to dissolve stand it in a warm place for a while, stirring now and again until lump-free. An extra precaution is to pass it through a sieve, muslin or jelly bag at the end

MARIGOLD SWISS VEGETABLE BOUILLON POWDER one of the best substitutes for fresh vegetable stock

TABASCO a very spicy sauce

BURGESS MUSHROOM KETCHUP use sparingly to add a rich brown colour and intense flavour

GARAM MASALA an Indian spice mixture

LEA & PERRINS WORCESTERSHIRE SAUCE an instant, piquant flavouring

LEA & PERRINS ROOT GINGER SAUCE use when fresh ginger is elusive

SOY SAUCE use the best quality, usually Japanese

SLITE OR SIMILAR PRODUCTS use like sugar; it contains half the calories as it is half artificial sweetener

STOCK CUBES invaluable, and I am no purist. Use them whenever stock is specified, in appropriate flavour, if you haven't any home-made in your freezer. Reduce salt used, however, as the stock cubes contain a lot

TUBS OF FRESH STOCK expensive but extremely good

'VERY LAZY' GARLIC sold in a jar

COCONUT 'MILK' use canned coconut milk, which is not the juice of the coconut but liquid extracted from the coconut flesh

It is useful to have in the store cupboard a variety of canned vegetables and fruits – unsweetened. Palm hearts, tomatoes, celery hearts and haricots verts are all very low-calorie standbys, for instance. Canned apples are brilliant for cooking purposes. Canned beef consommé is also very handy. Standard-sized cans are around 14 oz (400g) or 14 fl oz (400ml).

Equipment

The most useful equipment is your hands. After that, there is any amount of cooking equipment I could recommend. I am a sucker for kitchen gadgets and catalogues, and have addictive credit-card problems when in kitchen shops. I have to ration my outings. I am particularly drawn to beautiful copper pans, polythene containers and zinc objects for growing herbs and just to have.

What you use to cook with is an individual matter. The fact is that you could do most things by hand with a wooden spoon, a frying pan and a bonfire, if you wanted to.

However, here is an abbreviated list of things in the kitchen that I find most useful and which I think you'll need if you are going to try my recipes:

A reliable oven and hob, which you need to know well – I use an Aga, an electric cooker (our village doesn't have mains gas), and a 650-watt microwave. But they all have their ways, the Aga in particular, which tends to go out when I'm abroad. (This is true and whoever is in charge at home rings me up in despair, as it also heats the water. I still love it, though.)

Constantly sharpened, best quality kitchen knives of sizes and shapes to suit your hands and a 'Chantry' knife sharpener, which will last you the whole of your cooking life.

Kitchen scissors (snip your herbs with them in a mug, bacon to make 'lardons' and thousands of other tasks).

A collection of heavy-based saucepans with lids made of whatever metal is best for your cooker.

A wok with a lid: when I bought mine, which is big and made of stainless steel, I thought it an extravagance to be kept private. It's been worth its weight in gold.

Several good quality baking trays and roasting pans.

Very good quality oven-to-hob-to-table casserole pots in convenient

sizes. Cast iron, such as *Le Creuset*, though costly, is worth it: it lasts
forever.

Aluminium foil, non-stick baking paper (Bake-O-Glide is best and
can be reused over and over) and appropriate 'clingwraps'.

Non-stick frying pans – small, medium and large. Be prepared to
throw them away when they lose their non-stick capacity, as they
do in time.

A two-tier steamer.

Pyrex measuring jugs of different sizes, that will also go in a
microwave or low oven.

Tongs for turning things over and picking out to taste-test.

Slotted spoons and a sieve spoon.

Kitchen paper, for automatically and as a matter of habit, blotting off
excess fat.

Sieves, including a conical one, colanders and muslin. Plastic sieves are
needed for acidic fruits.

A good balloon whisk.

A rotary grater, meant for Parmesan but useful for many other things,
and nail-saving.

A juice squeezer that incorporates a pip retainer.

At least a hand-held electric beater/whisk, but preferably a proper
processor. I have two and one is a super stainless steel, all-systems-
go Magimix, a birthday present from Nigel. But what I use most in
everyday life is a small, inexpensive version made by Braun, which
my mother gave me. It has beaters, and will also chop and liquidise.

Accurate kitchen scales.

Quantities

The recipes in this book are generally enough for a family of four but sometimes that rule doesn't make sense – if, for instance, you are cooking a whole leg of lamb or doing smoked salmon mousse for a dinner party, so on those occasions I have given appropriate quantities.

As for amounts to allow for when shopping, it is not only useful to have guidelines in your head – especially when entertaining in numbers – but from the point of view of a dieter, it is a very good idea not to cook enough for regular second or third helpings.

As a rule, then, allow per person:

SOUP ¼ pint (150ml)

FISH ½ lb (225g) if on the bone; 6 oz (175g) if not

MEAT 4–6 oz (110–175g), when carved

RICE 1½–2 oz (40–50g) dry weight if it is the main component of the dish

PASTA 2–3 oz (50–75g) dry weight or 4–6 oz (110–175g) fresh, a bit on the mean side, but this *is* a diet book

Quality

It is not invariably the case that you get what you pay for, and no more with food than anything else. But with food you usually do have to pay more for certain types of quality. The most obvious example is that of organic food. Another current controversy is about beef on the bone: I desperately wanted to include my recipe for oxtail stew, one of Nigel's absolute favourites, but it became illegal while I was busy writing up my recipes.

I can speak only for myself. I certainly do not want to grow my own children with artificial substances; it hurts me to spend precious time, care and money on indifferent tasting foods; it disgusts me to deal with poultry that has been produced in unkind ways simply for its cheap protein value. But I recognise that modern methods of food production have also resulted in broadly safer and vastly varied food for more people. It is such a personal matter. If you can afford it, though, the cooking advice has to be 'go for the very best and certainly the freshest available'.

Cooking and Moods

Other people remember useful facts – events by their dates or venues, or by what they wore – and recall other people's names too, lucky things. I am not very good at these helpful social skills, but remember with often uncomfortable accuracy the emotional background to events and, of course, the food.

Just as there are times when you really need to go out, or have scrambled eggs in your nightie in front of the telly rather than cook a proper meal, so there are times when cooking is destined for unhappiness. Making hollandaise sauce is known in our household for being a barometer of 'her' temper: 99% of the time it works perfectly and I can do it in my sleep, though we have it much less often these days. On occasions, however, if something – or more plausibly, someone – has got under my skin, the sauce curdles and no amount of extra egg yolk, water or skill can rescue it. This does not help the out–of–sorts mood in the least bit.

Unfortunately, the first time I met John Major coincided with just such a scene. It must have been in 1987. We were living at Number Eleven and as the flat was 'above the shop' Nigel frequently brought people in for a drink, who then stayed for supper. I was nominally all for this – his visitors tended to be fascinating people and I liked the idea of being an open-house type. This particular evening someone he described as an 'excellent new addition' to his Treasury team was the

Post-diet Nigel at home in Northamptonshire with the family, including Cosima, one of his four grandchildren

victim. I had things on my mind and was irritated, but as I was about to embark on a pasta supper for my children, I accepted the extra guest. I shouldn't have: the angel-hair spaghetti turned into the nastiest congealed lumps of worms, the minced beef in the sauce looked like discoloured and mis-shapen meat balls, and I could have cried. To make things worse, a newish puppy (old enough, however, to know better) disgraced himself by the door that separated the flat from the State Rooms of Number Eleven. I shall not name the culprit for the sake of his dignity. This was really my fault for not taking the dogs out at the right time, due to the hurry over supper. The obligation to seem cheerful deserted me at this point and I went off to sulk in bed.

Anyway, Nigel's guest didn't stay long after eating and I just wished I'd been mature enough to say 'no' in the first place, rather than have allowed myself to get into such a mess. No great harm done in the long run, though. We became quite good friends and he was courteous enough never to mention his first supper at Number Eleven.

All the same, older as I certainly am and wiser as I now must be, surely, I recommend a take-away if you feel a bad mood coming on.

Starters and Salads

First courses are often the best part of the meal, partly because you eat them at your hungriest. It is also, though, because they lend themselves to creative and delicate presentation which is not so easy with main-course meat or fish.

Beware of thinking of starters as 'appetisers', for obvious reasons. Neither should they be uncomfortably gut-swelling: it is a good idea anyway for slimmers to avoid that rather distasteful state.

I have included a few salads in this section. I did not want to put salads on their own because I suspect I'm not alone in having to suppress a sigh at the notion that slimmers are obliged to overdose on leaves – you can have too much of a green thing.

If anything made me change my mind it would be the experiences at Shrubland Hall, the health clinic my friend Susan Crosland and I visit annually. I must admit I become panic-peckish whenever I am away from home and my own fridge, but at Shrublands I have learned that the variety of salads you can come up with is as expansive as your imagination – they can be filling and piquant or light and refreshing; not all of them are green by any means and they don't have to bear any resemblance to rabbit food. Nevertheless, salads should be kept in perspective and tend to feel more suitable in hot weather.

Mozzarella Wheels

I first sampled these titbits at the Villa d'Este on Lake Como, which is a most beautiful hotel in a fabulous location. Various conferences have been held there to which spouses have been invited – a stroke of good fortune for me: the food is a prime example of excellent Italian cooking.

Mine is a simplified version but the wheels make a most attractive first course that you can get ready well before take-off (see photograph).

MAKES 10 SMALL WHEELS

4¹/₂ oz (125g) buffalo Mozzarella	Drain the lump of Mozzarella and melt to soften until it is pliable, either in a microwave oven on a defrost setting for about 5 minutes or in a double boiler on top of the stove.
	When pliable, spread the Mozzarella in a thin layer about 8 x 6 inches (20 x 15cm) on clingwrap covering a kitchen board. Fiddle with the cheese until it is a regular oblong – you can pull and stretch the cheese like plasticine or use a clean empty milk bottle to roll it out.
1 dessertspoon ready-made fresh pesto	Then spread the pesto over it, using the substantial bit and not the oil it comes in.
4 slices prosciutto or Parma ham	Lay the ham slices evenly over the pesto, then the basil leaves and finally grind over some pepper.
10–12 fresh basil leaves	Roll the whole thing up carefully, starting from the shorter side and rolling up the length like a Swiss roll, to make a sausage shape.
pepper	Wrap tightly in a clean piece of clingwrap and screw up the ends so it looks like a cracker. Refrigerate for at least a couple of hours. When ready to serve, remove

the clingwrap and slice the roll into wheels: you should
get 10 or so.

a little tomato coulis (see recipe for *Tomato Sauce* on page 132) extra basil leaves, to decorate	Arrange prettily on individual plates spooning a small amount of the tomato coulis in between each wheel. Decorate with basil leaves.

Duck and Apricot Parfait

Not only does this parfait (see photograph) make a substantial first course for a dinner party, but you could equally well have it for lunch or supper. It keeps well in the fridge – useful for occasions when you have neither the time nor inclination to cook.

You can vary the main ingredients to suit: chicken livers alone or with chicken meat or bacon bits make a lovely pâté and so do pig livers with very lean pork. You can also vary the texture to make a rougher, 'country' pâté.

You will need a 1 pint (600ml) loaf tin, lined with foil for easier turning-out.

SERVES 6–8 AS A FIRST COURSE

1 boned duck breast	Preheat the oven to 200°C (400°F, Gas 6, Aga top oven). Prick the skin of the duck all over. Roast it on a rack for 15–20 minutes. Remove, but leave the oven on at the same temperature for cooking the parfait later. Wrap in a wad of kitchen paper and blot off excess fat. When cool enough to handle, strip off the skin. Carve the flesh into smallish cubes.

14 oz (400g) can of apricots in fruit juice	Drain the can of apricots, reserving 1 tablespoon of the juice.
1 medium-sized onion	Remove 2 apricot halves and reserve the rest for decoration later.
1 garlic clove	
a 9 oz (250g) tub frozen chicken livers, defrosted and drained	Peel and chop the onion and garlic.
1 tablespoon Grand Marnier	Liquidise or process the duck, onion, garlic, liver, Grand Marnier, egg, fromage frais, salt and pepper with the 2 apricots and the tablespoon of juice until you have a very smooth mixture, which will be runny, like a thin cream.
1 egg	
2–3 tablespoons virtually fat-free fromage frais	Pour into the loaf tin.
salt and pepper	Stand the loaf tin in a roasting pan. Pour warm water into the roasting pan until it comes halfway up the loaf tin.

Cook in the preheated oven for 25 minutes and then at 170°C (325°F, Gas 3, Aga simmer oven) for 1–1½ hours – a little longer in the Aga. Check for doneness after an hour by sticking a skewer in the middle: the juices should run clear when the parfait is cooked. You may need to cover the parfait with foil if it is going at all crusty on top.

the reserved apricot halves, halved again	Let the parfait stand until cool enough to handle. Then pour off any excess liquid.
watercress, rocket or other salad leaves of choice	Put a serving plate on top of it, invert, and carefully remove the foil.
	Chill until firm.
bread for toasting or wheat wafers, oatcakes etc	When ready to serve, decorate with apricots and surround with leaves of choice.
	Serve with hot toast or biscuits. Butter is not necessary.

Tomato Jelly with Quails' Eggs

Auseful and quite party-ish dish (see photograph) and not too tricky to achieve, especially if you stick to individual jellies. It is also good for lunch with plenty of salad for strict dieters.

Prepare well in advance to allow plenty of time for the jelly to set. You will need a 1 pint (600ml) ring mould, or six individual moulds holding at least 3 fl oz (75ml) each.

SERVES 6 AS A FIRST COURSE

1 pint (600ml) *Tomato Sauce* made without the olives (see recipe on page 132) 3 extra shakes of Tabasco	Push the sauce through a sieve and discard any debris left in the sieve. Measure the result. You need just under a pint (say 18 fl oz, 510ml). If there isn't enough, make up the quantity with tomato juice and/or water. Add the Tabasco.
1 sachet of powdered gelatine	Heat about a quarter of the sauce in a saucepan. When just bubbling, take off the heat. Leave for a minute, then sprinkle over the gelatine. Stir briskly with a metal spoon until dissolved. Add the rest of the sauce and stand in a warm place, stirring now and again, until you are satisfied that the jelly mixture is globule-free. Push through the sieve again into a jug and pour into the ring mould or individual dishes. Leave to cool.
6 quails' eggs salt	Boil the quails' eggs with salt: 2–3 minutes for hard, 1–2 minutes for soft. Plunge into cold water. When cool, peel very carefully: they are delicate to handle.

Place the eggs, evenly spaced, into the ring mould of jelly, or one in each individual pot.

Refrigerate until set (at least 4 hours).

---

1 large courgette

When you are nearly ready to serve the jelly, take the mould out of the fridge, dip into very hot water for 30 seconds only, put your serving plate on top and invert carefully, giving it a firm shake. This is a tricky operation. Keep your nerve, and good luck. (Of course, if you are serving the jelly in individual pots, you don't have to undergo the turning-out ordeal.)

Refrigerate the jelly again, while you prepare the courgette topping:

Blanch the courgette by plunging it into boiling water and standing for 5 minutes. Drain, dry well, and chop into 6 pieces.

Pulse-process the courgette in a processor so that you can control the result. You want firm crumbs to emerge in two shades of green – the inside and the peel.

2¹/₂ oz (60g) very low-fat yoghurt

pepper

1 plum tomato skinned and chopped (optional)

Remove the jelly from the fridge.

Sprinkle the courgette crumbs all over it.

Put the yoghurt in the middle of the jelly and grind pepper over it. Add tiny chunks of tomato, if you like.

Asparagus with Lemon, Shaved Parmesan and Citrus Pepper (v)

So delicious is English asparagus, at its plumpest and most yielding in late May, that there is no need for complicated treatment. I try to arrange for that time of year my annual pilgrimage to Shrublands Health Clinic, near Ipswich, because the Suffolk asparagus is simply fabulous then and very reasonably priced in the farm shops.

Shrublands is half about losing weight, of course. (The other half is to do with 'well-being' and catching up with the gossip.) It is entirely appropriate to come home from our renewing week with bundles and bundles of asparagus in the car, since it is remarkably low in calories (25 per 100g). Therefore, dieters should treat themselves to as much as they can afford and get their hands on.

This is the way I like it most:

SERVES 2–4

1 lb (450g) English asparagus	Cut off any woody stalks and make the lengths of asparagus even. Use a potato peeler to remove any tough bits on the stems.
salt	
¹/₂ oz (10g) Parmesan cheese	Steam with a little salt until just done, probably about 10 minutes.
	Remove and drain, and arrange on plates.
	Shave Parmesan strips on top – just a few.
the juice of half a lemon	When ready to serve, mix the citrus pepper bits or black peppercorns into the lemon juice and sprinkle over the asparagus.
¹/₂ teaspoon crushed citrus pepper or black peppercorns	
	It is best to serve the asparagus *tiède* (lukewarm) and divide it between individual salad plates, otherwise not everyone gets their fair share, I have observed.

24-Hour Tomato Consommé (V)

T he idea for this recipe came from Hambleton Hall in Rutland, a hotel renowned for its fabulous food and comfort and, most fortunately, owned by a friend of mine. This version is an amateurish approximation but very popular at home.

It is a smart and delicate starter, or 'amuse-gueule'. You need to start to prepare it 24 hours in advance, but then it is not at all time consuming and is as easy as pie – and about a million times less calorific.

You will need a colander (stainless steel or plastic) that sits well on a bowl, or a sieve that fits over a jug.

SERVES 6

24 small, highly flavoured tomatoes, weighing about 1 lb (450g) 4 shallots 24 fresh basil leaves 1–2 teaspoons Slite 1 teaspoon Worcestershire sauce a shake of Tabasco 1 teaspoon salt	Skin the tomatoes and cut them in half. Peel the shallots and chop each one into 8 pieces. Roughly shred the basil leaves. Put all these ingredients with the flavourings in the colander or sieve, sitting on its receptacle.
¼ pint (150ml) boiling water	Pour over the boiling water. Cover, for hygiene, and leave to drip in a cool place for 24 hours, squashing the tomatoes every now and again with a wooden spoon to encourage the pulp to leak.
a 2-inch (5cm) piece of cucumber, peeled and cubed very finely	The next day when as much juice as possible has gone through, strain it through muslin or a jelly bag into a jug. It should be a clear yellowy-red colour.

Chill it in the jug.

Distribute the cucumber evenly between 6 small cups.

Stir the tomato essence and pour into the cups.

Give everyone a coffee spoon on their saucers, to scoop up
the cucumber dice.

NOTE: Don't throw away the pulp from the colander – it can be
used as the base for a strong, uncooked tomato coulis.

Buckwheat Blinis for Caviar and Other Treats

Just in case someone comes across with a bit of caviar (*osietra*, rather than *beluga*, is our favourite, by far), you need to know how to cook blinis. As caviar is far too expensive to eat in quantity it's unlikely to be fattening. Caviar is food for the angels except that it is also reputed to be aphrodisiac. Blinis are also good for piling on strips of smoked salmon, salmon caviar and a blob of sour cream for a smart-looking and delicious first course.

My children also like blinis, for tea with butter and blackcurrant jam, like drop scones in my day. The buckwheat flour you need does not always appear in supermarkets but you'll get it without too much trouble in a health food shop or similar. Doves Farm produce it, for instance. I used to use Aunt Jemima's Buckwheat Pancake Mix, which was wonderful but suddenly got withdrawn from the shelves here: I can't imagine why. My step-daughter, Nigella, who is extremely knowledgeable about food, got me some buckwheat flour and a blini pan and helped me make the pancakes from scratch.

I now make the blinis in a non-stick frying pan, 4 or 5 at a time, which helps to reduce the amount of oil needed.

MAKES ENOUGH FOR 50 SMALL BLINIS

7 oz (200g) buckwheat flour ¹/₂ teaspoon bicarbonate of soda 1 teaspoon cream of tartar ¹/₂ teaspoon salt	Sift the flour, bicarbonate of soda, cream of tartar and salt into a large bowl or the bowl of the processor.
2 eggs ¹/₂ pint (300ml) semi-skimmed milk	Add the eggs and mix into the flour. Then add the milk and vigorously mix everything until it is a smooth and slightly frothy batter. Stand for half an hour to an hour before cooking.
up to 1 dessertspoon sunflower or safflower oil	Heat a non-stick frying pan. Put in half the oil. Very carefully indeed, spoon a little pancake mix into the pan – about a tablespoonful at a time. You will soon get the hang of it: the first batch is usually not quite right. You want your blinis each to be 2–3 inches (5–7cm) in diameter. You can do 4–5 at a time in a normal-sized pan. Halfway through, you might need to add the rest of the oil. As you take the blinis out, put them on a small baking tray lined with a double thickness of kitchen paper to blot off excess oil. Slip out the kitchen paper at the end and reheat the blinis in a low oven until you are ready to go, but be careful not to over-crisp them.

Fennel and Orange Salad

Fennel is perhaps an acquired taste, being aniseedy. I would not necessarily expect this to be a children's favourite, but it is wonderfully healthy, good for water-retention problems, I believe, and crisp and refreshing.

This salad would be best on a hot day for lunch with cold, poached salmon – fennel and fish is a happy combination.

It was because of my first father-in-law, Peter Medawar, a genius, that I learned among other things, a better way to peel oranges. After his tragic stroke, which occurred in his prime during a lecture he was delivering in a cathedral – he always said that it served him right for meddling with the supernatural, as he was a rationalist to a fault – he was unable to perform acts such as peeling oranges, which he greatly liked after Sunday lunch. It was frequently I, his temporary daughter-in-law, who got the job. I found it tricky every time, and the smell of orange peel seemed to linger under my nails until Wednesday. Now I know better.

This is **how to peel oranges** with less hassle. The method works with grapefruits, lemons, tomatoes, nectarines and many other fruits and vegetables, including onions.

- Put the oranges in a large bowl in the sink.
- Pour copious amounts of boiling water over them.
- Leave for a minute or two at the most.
- Run cold water over them until they have cooled.
- Score with a sharp knife from top to bottom in 4 places.
- They will now peel readily, and the white pith, which looks and tastes horrible, will come off as well.

SERVES 4 AS AN ACCOMPANIMENT

1 fennel bulb	Trim the fennel bulb, top and bottom. Chop into neat cubes. Blanch the fennel in boiling water for 30 seconds, plunge into cold water and drain thoroughly. Pat dry with kitchen paper.
2 large juicy oranges 1 tablespoon orange juice the juice of half a lemon pepper salt	Peel the oranges (see above), segment and chop into small chunks. Arrange the fennel and orange attractively in a salad dish. Pour over the orange and lemon juices and grind over the pepper. Sprinkle lightly with salt.

Dark Green Astringent Salad (V)

This recipe is my concession to 'rabbit food' and a far cry from it too – it is a good-looking, sharp leaf salad and by far the family favourite (see photograph).

SERVES 4

4½ oz (125g) baby spinach leaves 2 oz (50g) watercress 2 oz (50g) rocket (preferably 'wild')	Prepare all the salad leaves, rinsing only if you have to, and cut off any stalks. Blot very gently in kitchen paper. Combine in a salad bowl.
⅓ of a Bramley apple, peeled	Using a potato peeler, shave apple wafers into a separate bowl. Toss with a few drops of lemon juice to prevent

a little lemon juice	discolouration. Add the apple wafers to the salad bowl.

2 tablespoons cider or apple vinegar	Mix together the vinegar, oil and Slite.
1½ tablespoons hazelnut or walnut oil	Add to the bowl and, preferably using your fingers, turn the leaves over gently but thoroughly in the dressing, aiming to get all of them glossy.
1 scant teaspoon of Slite	Add salt and pepper, if required.
salt and pepper, to taste	Serve immediately.

Broad Bean and 'Bacon' Salad

For this salad, you need to have made a *Slimmers' Parsley Sauce* first (see page 130). It is particularly nice with ham or cold chicken, or both. Serve it at room temperature rather than straight from the fridge, otherwise the dressing will be too thick and the flavour frozen.

SERVES 4 AS AN ACCOMPANIMENT

2 lb (900g) unpodded fresh, young broad beans	Pod, then steam or boil the broad beans with salt until just soft – about 10 minutes.
salt	Plunge briefly into cold water and drain.
	When cool enough to handle, slip off their jackets.
	Put the beans in a salad bowl.

¼ pint (150ml) cold *Slimmers' Parsley Sauce* (see page 130)	Loosen the parsley sauce with the yoghurt and pour over the broad beans.
2 tablespoons very low-fat yoghurt	Mix the sauce and the beans together gently.

pepper	Sprinkle with pepper and 'bacon' chips or bacon.
a handful of soya 'bacon' chips or 2 rashers of streaky bacon, crisped and crumbled	

Raw Beetroot and Grapefruit Salad

The only spot of bother I had with the publisher of this book was over beetroot. She, the publisher, maintains that she herself likes it, but I've noticed that each beetroot recipe I've come up with has met with a bit of resistance.

I, however, love growing beetroot in my self-indulgent, small vegetable patch: their leaves are so pretty with their red veins and deep green colour and are delicious cooked like spinach. It's particularly satisfying to be able to pull out root vegetables and, depending on the condition of the soil, the beetroot can vary in taste.

So, not to be deflected, here is a recipe for fresh raw beetroot salad, which is brilliantly low in calories, and tastes really lovely.

SERVES 4 AS AN ACCOMPANIMENT

4 small, fresh, raw beet-root, weighing 8–10 oz (225–275g)	Peel, top and tail the beetroot. Grate or shred them in a processor. Roll the beetroot shreds around gently in muslin or kitchen paper to eliminate excess moisture.
1 large, juicy grapefruit (pink for preference)	Peel the grapefruit using the method described for oranges on page 35. Segment and chop into smallish pieces,

saving any juice and picking off the membrane and pips:
a bit fiddly.

Put the grapefruit in a bowl with any saved juice.

---

the juice of half a lime
1 tablespoon unsweet-
   ened grapefruit juice
   (optional)
a little salt and pepper

Add the beetroot and disperse evenly and attractively. Do
this at the last minute, or the beetroot will leak into the
grapefruit.

Sprinkle over the lime juice, extra grapefruit juice if you
like, and salt and pepper.

Soups,
Hot and Cold

S oups are very useful indeed for would-be slim people. They are comfort food in winter, for a start, and very filling: a lunch comprising a large bowl of soup followed by an imaginative salad is ideal if you plan a proper dinner for the evening. Equally, cold soups in summer are refreshing and perfect food for alfresco lunches.

Soups are also a useful way of getting healthy vegetables down people, often children, who don't like to see the real thing on their plate. By and large, also, the ingredients needed are inexpensive.

The way to make soups less fattening is to eliminate the usual first step of sweating the ingredients in butter: you can achieve a fine result by fast-boiling in a little liquid to start off. Then you can substitute low-fat yoghurt for the quantities of cream that many recipes for soups include.

Served with *Fatless Croûtons* (see recipe on page 53), these soups will take the edge off anybody's hunger.

Unpeeled Artichoke Soup

J erusalem artichokes have a lovely and distinctive flavour, quite sub-
tle though, which is the reason for spicing up the soup with curry
flavour and plenty of salt and pepper.
People get put off these vegetables thinking that the preparation is
too fiddly, and that you have to deal with all their knobbly protuber-
ances and peel around them. It isn't necessary: so long as you scrub
them a bit, you can leave on the peel, which will add to the nutritional value as well as the taste. The same goes for the new potatoes.

SERVES 6–8

2 lb (900g) Jerusalem artichokes	Scrub the artichokes and trim off the rough ends. Slice into discs.
3 new potatoes, weighing about 3 oz (75g)	Scrub the potatoes and cut in half. Peel the onions and chop roughly.
2 medium-sized onions	Top and tail the carrots and slice into discs.
2 large carrots	
2 pints (1.2 litres) strong *Vegetable Stock* (see page 127)	Bring the stock to the boil with the vegetables. Simmer until the vegetables are tender – about 30 minutes. Skim off any scum with a sieve spoon or slotted spoon. Remove the vegetables, either with a slotted spoon, or using a colander and draining the liquid into a bowl. Process the vegetables until completely smooth with about ¼ pint (150ml) of the liquid.
1 heaped teaspoon garam masala salt and pepper, to taste	Return all the liquid and the vegetables to the pan, add the seasonings and reheat gently for 5 minutes, stirring until the soup is smooth and hot. Add boiling water if you think the soup is too thick. Taste and adjust seasoning if necessary.

1 tablespoon very finely
chopped watercress
leaves or fresh parsley

To serve, garnish with watercress or parsley.

Hot Beetroot Soup

I looked up '*bortsch*' in *Larousse Gastronomique* out of curiosity. Apparently a version presented to the Court of St Petersburg by Carême (a penniless Parisian who became chef to the Rothschilds in the 1800s) needed, among other things, a duck, a chicken, sausages, bacon, minced beef, four ounces of pure fat – and a whole oxtail to garnish.

My recipe is totally dissimilar and certainly less fattening.

SERVES 4–6

8 small beetroot (vacuum-
packed is acceptable if
you can't get fresh
beetroot, which is
however always nicer)

If using raw beetroot, rinse well and cook in enough water to cover them until tender – about 40 minutes.
Drain, plunge into cold water and peel: the skin comes off very easily.
Chop each cooked beetroot into 4 pieces.

2 large leeks
1 pint (600ml) or more
Vegetable Stock (see
page 127)
salt and pepper
3 tablespoons very low-
fat yoghurt

Trim the leeks and slice into thin discs. Wash thoroughly.
Blend the raw leeks and cooked beetroot in the processor with a little of the stock.
Put the mushed vegetables and the rest of the stock in a saucepan and bring slowly to the boil.
Add more water if the result is more like a purée than a soup, but don't expect a completely smooth texture as the leeks remain bitty, being barely cooked.
Simmer for 5 minutes, stirring all the time.
Season to taste, take off the heat and stir in the yoghurt.

43

Sweet Chestnut Soup

Nuts are notoriously fattening due mainly to their high oil content – not a good idea for pre-lunch nibbles. Thankfully, chestnuts are at the bottom end of the nut calorie scale; you can use the frozen, vacuum-packed or canned peeled chestnuts that have no added sugar, and make the soup without butter. It is very rich, thick and sweet: a little goes a long way.

Chestnut soup is good for an autumn supper party. In this recipe I have included a leaf vegetable, which turns the soup green and surprises its recipients who are expecting vegetable soup but taste the smooth sweetness of chestnut. If you don't like that idea, you can leave out the leaves.

SERVES 8 OR MORE

2¹/₄ pints (1.35 litres) *Vegetable Stock* (see page 127)	Reserve ³/₄ pint (425ml) of the stock. Put the remaining stock into a lidded saucepan with the chestnuts, onions and apple pieces.
1 lb (450g) prepared peeled chestnuts with no additives	Bring to the boil over a medium heat, turn right down and put on the lid.
1 medium-sized onion, peeled and chopped	Simmer very gently for 15 minutes.
2 oz (50g) unsweetened dried apple rings or canned apple slices	
3 oz (75g) shredded spring greens or cabbage leaves (optional)	Stir in the greens, if using. Simmer for another 15 minutes. Cool a little, liquidise the soup and return to the pan.
the reserved vegetable stock	Thin the soup to your liking with the rest of the stock and adjust seasoning while reheating.
salt and pepper	

Rustic Celeriac Soup

The smell of celeriac invariably evokes in me memories of that huge and utterly rural space on the South West French side of the Pyrenees where in summer nothing, not even the air, seems to move. I first cooked celeriac there, in my long-distant youth, copying the busy housewives preparing huge lunches: the place always smelled of celeriac by noon.

Mashed Celeriac (see recipe on page 120) is particularly good with game, to soak up the gravy. Celeriac chips are excellent too. Raw and grated, celeriac also makes a lovely salad, especially with apple. Best of all its uses, in my opinion, is in this soup, although it is a rather murky country colour. It benefits from a little butter and oil, so this time don't leave them out.

SERVES 6–8

---

1 medium-sized celeriac, weighing about 1 lb (450g)
1 teaspoon lemon juice
8 oz (225g) potatoes
1 large carrot

Prepare the celeriac. They are tough old boots: cut off the thick outer layer then cut the root into 16 pieces and sprinkle over a little lemon juice straight away, or they will discolour.
Scrub the potatoes and carrot and chop into pieces roughly the same size as the celeriac.

---

3 celery sticks
the stalks of spring greens or broccoli, if available – about 3 heaped tablespoons, when chopped
1 large onion, weighing about 6 oz (175g)
1 garlic clove (optional)

Blanch the celery sticks in boiling water for 1 minute. Drain, and pull off any stringy lengths. Reserve one whole stick for garnishing and chop the rest into largish bits.
Chop up the stalks of the greens.
Peel and roughly chop the onion.
Peel and slice the garlic, if using.

---

¹/₂ oz (10g) butter
1 dessertspoon olive oil
	Melt the butter and oil over a medium heat in a large
	    heavy-based saucepan with a lid.
	Put in all the vegetables and turn them about in the pan for
	    a few minutes.
	Turn down the heat, put on the lid and let the vegetables
	    sweat for 5–10 minutes, but avoid browning them.

2 pints (1.2 litres) hot,
    strong *Vegetable Stock*
    (see page 127)
	Add 1¹/₂ pints (850ml) of the stock, reserving the rest. Bring
	    everything to simmering point, put the lid back on and
	    cook gently until all the vegetables are tender – about
	    30 minutes.
	Take off the heat and leave to stand for a bit.
	When lukewarm, process. It will end up fairly smooth, but
	    not velvety, and very thick.

the reserved vegetable
    stock
salt and pepper
the reserved celery stick
	Return to the saucepan. Reheat gently, add as much of the
	    reserved stock to thin as you think is right, taste and
	    season appropriately.
	To serve, dice the reserved celery very finely and sprinkle
	    onto the soup.

Apple and Parsnip Soup

Curried parsnip soup is a delicious old favourite – Jane Grigson has a lovely recipe in her *Good Things* – but this combination of apple and parsnip is also very pleasing, both savoury and sweetish, especially when you add a little coconut milk. Curiously, I first had it at a Midlands Woman of the Year Luncheon, which I anticipated with some foreboding but in the event enjoyed immensely. Kind neighbours took me when we first moved to Northamptonshire from London.

SERVES 4−6

1 medium-sized onion	Peel the onion and chop into large chunks.
1 medium-sized apple	Do the same with the apple, carrot and parsnips.
1 large carrot	Heat the juice in a large saucepan with a lid and add the
4 medium-sized parsnips	apple and vegetables.
¼ pint (150ml) unsweetened apple juice	Turn them around on a high heat until almost all of the juice has evaporated.

1½ pints (850ml) hot, strong *Vegetable Stock* (see page 127)	Add the stock, bring to the boil, cover and simmer until the vegetables are tender – about 15–20 minutes.
salt and pepper, to taste	Take off the heat and, using a slotted spoon, put the solids into a liquidiser and process until quite smooth.
2 fl oz (55ml) canned coconut milk (optional)	Return the purée to the saucepan, stir and season according to taste.
	Add the coconut milk at the last minute if you want a velvety soup.

Chicken and Fennel Soup

Chicken and fennel is a truly delicious combination and this soup emerges smooth and creamy, thanks to the inclusion of the egg and lemon liaison at the end.

SERVES 6

1 fennel bulb
1 pint (600ml) strong
   Poultry Stock (see
   page 128)
4 new potatoes, weighing
   about 4 oz (110g)
	Trim the fennel and then chop coarsely, reserving the fennel fronds for use later. Bring the stock to the boil, add the fennel and simmer for 10 minutes.
	Scrub the potatoes, cut into 1-inch pieces if large, then add to the pan and continue simmering until they are just done.
	Put everything in the liquidiser and process – but not too much. You want some bits to remain.

1 chicken stock cube (optional) salt and pepper	Reheat the soup to a rolling boil and taste: this is when you need to decide whether to add water and/or a stock cube, salt and pepper.
1 egg the juice of half a lemon	Break the egg into a bowl and whisk in the lemon juice.

the reserved fennel
   fronds or 1 dessert-
   spoon chopped parsley
julienne strips of cooked
   chicken (optional)
	Snip the reserved fennel fronds with scissors. Take the pan off the heat and whisk in the egg and lemon mixture.
	Serve sprinkled with the fennel or parsley, and the chicken, if using.

Fragrant Spinach Soup

Ordinary spinach (or sorrel, or a mixture of both) makes a great soup, hot or cold, but this version is nice for a change with its oriental touch. Dark green soups look lovely too (see photograph).

SERVES 10

2½ pints (1.5 litres) *Vegetable Stock* (see page 127) 1 medium-sized potato 1 medium-sized onion	Reserve 1½ pints (850ml) of the stock and bring the remaining pint (600ml) to the boil. Scrub the potato and cut into 4 pieces. Peel the onion and chop into 8 pieces. Cook the potato and onion in the stock for 10 minutes.
1 bag of spinach, weighing 9 oz (250g) the reserved vegetable stock	Rinse the spinach, then pick over by hand, discarding any tough stalks. Add the spinach to the pan and cook on a low heat for a few minutes, until the spinach is wilted and the potatoes yield nicely to the point of a knife. When cool enough to liquidise, do so. Return to the pan. Add and amalgamate as much of the rest of the stock as suits for the final result.
a good piece, about 1 inch (2.5cm) square, of fresh root ginger, peeled and grated salt and pepper	While gently reheating, add the ginger, salt and pepper. Taste for seasoning, after allowing five minutes for the flavours to mingle properly. Adjust and reliquidise, if necessary.
a 14 fl oz (400ml) can of coconut milk 1 tablespoon fresh coriander, chopped	Remove from the heat and stir in the coriander and 4 fl oz (120ml) of the coconut milk, reserving the rest.

the reserved coconut milk	To serve, ladle into bowls, swirl a spoonful of coconut milk
2 tablespoons desiccated coconut	on top and sprinkle over a little desiccated coconut and soya 'bacon' chips if you like.
2 oz (50g) soya 'bacon' chips (optional)	

NOTE:	It is easy to grate root ginger if it is frozen and anyway it is useful to have it available in the freezer.

Gazpacho

This soup, served ice-cold, is Spanish in origin. You will not want much at a time, partly because it feels right only on a very hot day, when in any case no one wants too much food. Raw vegetables, I feel sure, are immensely good for you but at the same time too many all at once can be upsetting for the system.

That said, at the right time gazpacho is absolutely delicious and not at all fattening done in this way. The proper version includes a substantial amount of olive oil.

SERVES 8–12

1 large cucumber	Peel and top and tail the cucumber and courgettes. Slice
2 large green courgettes	into discs.
1/2 a leek	Slice the leek into thin discs, and rinse off any grit. Dry well
salt	in kitchen paper.
	Put all these vegetables into a bowl, sprinkle over a little salt, cover with kitchen paper and leave for at least 30 minutes. This allows them to sweat off excess moisture and any bitterness. Blot them with the paper before using.

5 large plum tomatoes	Put the tomatoes in a very large bowl in the sink.
1 small red pepper	Cut the pepper lengthways into 4, cut out the pith and seeds and add to the tomatoes in the bowl.
	Pour copious amounts of boiling water over the tomatoes and pepper and leave to stand for 5 minutes. Then turn on the cold tap and run the water over the vegetables until cool. Drain.
	Skin the tomatoes and dry the pepper pieces in kitchen paper.
1 bunch of spring onions	Trim the spring onions, discarding most of the green tops.
2 plump garlic cloves	Slice the rest into discs.
2 shallots	Peel and chop the garlic cloves and shallots.
12 pitted black olives	Put all the prepared vegetables in the processor. (It is possible that you will need to do this in 2 batches, depending on the size of your machine.)
1 teaspoon Tabasco or more, to taste	
1 dessertspoon Worcestershire sauce	Add the olives and then the spicy seasonings, vodka, if using, and other liquids.
1/4 pint (150ml) vodka (optional)	Process until the gazpacho is thick and soupy, but retains plenty of crunch.
1/4 pint (150ml) water	
the juice of half a lemon	
1/2 pint (300ml) unsweet-ened tomato juice	
a lot of black pepper	
salt, to taste	
ice	To serve, crush some ice cubes in a polythene bag, using a rolling pin. Put in the bottom of each bowl.
1 oz (25g) fresh parsley, finely chopped	Ladle out a small portion of gazpacho for each person.
Fatless Croûtons (see recipe on page 53)	Sprinkle the parsley over evenly.
	Serve with 4 or 5 croûtons per bowl.

Mango, Carrot and Stilton Soup

This is definitely a summer soup and is lovely for a light and very healthy lunch in the garden on a really hot day, followed by a large salad. You will want only a little as it is thick and strongly flavoured.

SERVES 8

1 ripe mango	Cut the mango in half lengthways, remove the stone, and scoop out the flesh with a spoon.
2 medium-sized carrots	
4 oz (110g) fresh pineapple, peeled and chopped, or from a can of chunks in natural juice	Peel the carrots and chop roughly.
	Put all the ingredients, except 1–2 fl oz (25–55ml) of the carrot juice, into the processor and whizz until smooth.
3 tablespoons very low-fat yoghurt	
½ pint (300ml) water	
½ pint (300ml) carrot juice (available in cartons)	
the juice of a lemon	
1 teaspoon ginger sauce	
a little salt	Season to taste, adding more carrot juice, or pineapple juice from the can, if the soup seems too thick.
a lot of pepper	
2–4 oz (50–110g) Stilton or Dolcelatte cheese, to taste	To serve, melt the cheese in a double boiler, or in a bowl set over a saucepan of boiling water, or in the microwave on low for a minute or so.
	Swirl a little into each bowl of soup.

Fatless Croûtons (V)

Proper croûtons, fried in butter, are delicious – precisely because of the large amount of butter the little cubes of bread absorb. Fatless ones are not so exciting, but they are, nevertheless, very nice and many soups benefit from having a few crunchy morsels crop up now and again.

All you do is preheat the oven to 180°C (350°F, Gas 4, or use the baking oven of the Aga) and cut off the crusts from a chunk of good, unsliced bread. Keep the crusts to make breadcrumbs. Then cut the bread into small cubes, no bigger than half an inch (1cm) each.

Lay them in a single layer on a baking tray and bake in a medium oven until dried out and lightly browned – about 20-30 minutes. Cool and store in plastic bags until needed.

You can also make the croûtons on top of the stove, using a non-stick and ungreased frying pan, or even in a microwave oven set to high for between 3 and 5 minutes, but keep a watchful eye as breads differ in their density.

Light Meals

It is a fundamental principle of this eating plan that, by and large, you have only one high-protein-with-trimmings meal a day. I have termed those recipes 'proper dinners' (see page 93-114). On holiday and at other exceptional times, most of us diverge from this format, of course, but if applied usually, you are most unlikely to put back on the excess weight that you have lost. Certainly the formula has worked conclusively for Nigel, The Guinea Pig, over the past three years and more.

For similar reasons, it is wise not to have meat and cheese at the same meal as a habit: it is just too much rich and fattening food at once. But, once your weight is down, by all means sometimes have a cheese-based dish for one of your meals of the day. This sounds bossy, which I have tried to avoid being (not easy for me). I don't mean to *pre*scribe, but rather to *de*scribe the facts.

This chapter includes a few recipes for, as it were, the second meal of the day – several cheesy ones included. Cravings for cheese shouldn't always be ignored or you might feel miserable. A miserable dieter is far less likely to be a successful one.

Platter of Raw Meats and Fruits

This makes a pretty and perfectly delicious light meal, and is particularly suited to a summer's day lunch. It couldn't be easier to prepare and there is no actual cooking involved – a bonus in hot weather, especially if you have a hot Aga-kitchen or similar, as I do.

As it is generous with meat, it would be ideal to cook a fish, cheese or vegetable dish for dinner. If you can, use bresaola di cervo (air dried venison).

MAKES A PLATTER FOR I

2 thin slices bresaola or nearest equivalent 2 thin slices prosciutto 2 thin slices carpaccio	Arrange the 2 slices of bresaola prettily on an individual platter, curled loosely into wavy shapes. Place the other types of meat in the same style and equidistantly around the platter.
6 balls Charentais melon 6 balls watermelon 1 fresh fig, quartered	Place 4 melon balls in between each type of meat. In the middle, arrange the fig quarters.
pepper 1/2 oz (10g) Parmesan cheese	Sprinkle the pepper generously over the meats *and* fruits. Add a little Parmesan, shaved with a potato peeler, and curled into more waves.

Chicken and Mango Buffet Lunch

Y ou will need to use a wok or a large, lidded frying pan or casserole. You can serve this hot with rice, but it is most useful cold for a summer buffet luncheon, a change from the ubiquitous Coronation Chicken (now to be found in all brands of ready-mades and which I am bored with as it was a very regular feature on the menus of Conservative Party dos).

This version is less fattening because it uses very low-fat yoghurt instead of oil-laden mayonnaise.

SERVES 8–10

2 lb (900g) chicken breast, boned and skinned	Cut the chicken breasts into fine strips, about 3 inches (7cm) long and half an inch (1cm) thick.
2 medium-sized mangoes	Peel the mangoes, as you would for a potato. Then cut off as much flesh as you can and chop into cubes of about 1 inch (2.5cm). Reserve about a quarter of the mango cubes for garnishing.
1 medium-sized leek	Top, tail and slice the leek into thin discs. Rinse well and pat dry with kitchen paper.
1 tablespoon sesame oil	Heat the oil in the wok, frying pan or casserole over a high heat.
1 tablespoon Japanese soy sauce	Put the leek in and stir around.
2 tablespoons Green Thai Curry Paste (Bart Spices)	Add the chicken strips. Cook for 5 minutes until brown. Turn over and cook for another 3 minutes. Stir in the mango cubes, then the soy sauce. Add the Thai curry paste, mixing everything in well. Turn the heat down to minimum, put on the lid, and leave for 10 minutes.

Remove the pan from the heat and leave to cool, uncovered.

2 x 5 oz (150g) tubs very low-fat yoghurt 1 bunch of spring onions the reserved mango cubes pepper	To serve, arrange the chicken and mango in a serving dish. Stir in the yoghurt for dressing – you may not need to use all of it. Slice the spring onions very finely and pile on top of the dish with the reserved mango cubes. Grind over the pepper.

Luncheon Mushrooms

Mushrooms, of which there are endless varieties available, are usefully unfattening, but are sabotaged in this regard when cooked in loads of butter. This recipe cooks them mainly in liquids instead. You can vary the type of mushrooms depending on availability and preference – though I like ordinary big, flat field mushrooms best of all.

SERVES 2

2 tablespoons dried wild mushrooms of choice 3 fl oz (75ml) warm water	Soak the dried mushrooms in the water for at least 30 minutes. Drain and dry on kitchen paper, discarding the soaking liquor.
1 dessertspoon truffle oil (or hazelnut or olive oil) $\frac{1}{2}$ teaspoon coriander seeds, crushed with the pestle in the mortar	In a large 9–12 inch (23–30cm) non-stick frying pan, heat the oil and fry the coriander seeds for 1–2 minutes, without burning. Then add the fresh and wild mushrooms to the pan. Fry, stirring gently, until all is hot, then add the mushroom ketchup and lemon juice.

8 oz (225g) field mushrooms, sliced 1 tablespoon mushroom ketchup 1 tablespoon lemon juice salt and pepper 1 dessertspoon finely chopped coriander	Simmer, stirring all the time, until the mushrooms have become dark, soft and reduced – 10 minutes or more. Season to taste, and sprinkle in the fresh coriander.
2–4 slices hot toast	To serve, pile the mushrooms onto the toast and pour over all the juices. You do not need butter.

Hot Palm Hearts

This is one excuse to indulge in cheese sauce. Palm hearts make a nice change from celery or endive, and a virtue of this recipe is that the chances are you will have the ingredients in the store cupboard, as standbys, so can rustle it up quickly – it is very simple.

SERVES 2

1 pint (600ml) *Light Cheese Sauce* (see page 130) a 14 oz (400g) can of whole palm hearts 4 oz (110g) boiled ham, diced *or* 2 oz (50g) soya 'bacon' chips	Preheat the oven to 200°C (400°F, Gas 6, Aga top oven). Drain the palm hearts, pat dry with kitchen paper and lay them flat in a gratin dish. Sprinkle over the ham chunks or 'bacon' chips. Cover with the cheese sauce.
1 tablespoon grated Parmesan cheese pepper	Sprinkle with Parmesan and pepper. Bake for 20–30 minutes, until browned and bubbling.

Broccoli and Cauliflower Mustard-Cheese

A plain, old favourite this – and none the worse for that: a perfect telly evening supper. Because it is vegetable-based, it makes a good second meal of the day (see photograph).

SERVES 4

4 baby cauliflowers	Preheat the oven to 220°C (425°F, Gas 7, Aga top oven).
4 baby broccoli	Prepare the vegetables: discard any tough stalks but chop up the tender stalks and leaves and place them in the bottom tray of a double steamer.
	Put the cauliflowers and broccoli heads, intact, in the top tray.
	Salt lightly and steam until just cooked.
	Drain the cooked stalks and leaves well and then process them to a purée; reserve.
	Arrange the drained cauliflowers and broccoli heads in an ovenproof dish.
1 oz (25g) unsalted butter	Make a white sauce over a medium heat. Melt the butter in a heavy-based saucepan. Add the flour, and then the milk, a little at a time, stirring continuously with a wooden spoon, until the sauce is smooth and has bubbled for a few minutes.
1 tablespoon plain flour	
³/₄ pint (450ml) skimmed milk	

4¹/₂ oz (125g) half-fat Cheddar cheese, grated	Add the cheese and the Guinness, if using, and stir until mixed in.
a splash of Guinness (optional)	Finally, stir in the mustard powder, salt and pepper. Set aside in a warm place to thicken further.
2–3 tablespoons mustard powder, to taste	
salt and pepper	

the reserved stalk purée	Mix the stalk purée into the sauce. Then pour it over the cauliflowers and broccoli.
1 tablespoon grated Parmesan cheese	Sprinkle the Parmesan on top, and a little more pepper. Bake for about 25 minutes, until bubbling and brown.

Mushroom and Truffly 'Risotto'

This is, I am afraid, far from a classic risotto which demands large quantities of butter and cheese. It would be tragic, however, to dismiss forever the comfort of a soupy, flavoursome rice dish from a dieter's menu. So here is a compromise recipe which happily fits the bill.

The result that you're aiming for is a creamy, soft bowlful of rice with some bite, that you can eat with a fork: if you need a spoon, the risotto is just a bit too soupy but, on the other hand, it must not end up at all dry. A small piece of good, soft brown bread with seeds is the nicest way to soak up every little bit of liquor. Risotto is best served in large bowls. If you can run to it, shave white truffle over the dish. Or use truffle sauce, available in jars at good delicatessens.

It is best to make risotto when you can serve and eat it straightaway and, because you have to attend to it and stir rather assiduously throughout, it is perhaps jollier to have it with friends of the sort who will chat to you in the kitchen. There is, however, a way of keeping risotto warm, if you are obliged to prepare it a bit in advance: simply take it off the heat before you use the last two ladlefuls of stock, then add the stock (but don't stir it in), mushrooms and cheeses, put on the lid and keep the pan in a warmer or in the oven at the lowest possible setting. Stir at the end.

SERVES 4 FOR LUNCH OR 6–8 AS A FIRST COURSE

1 good handful of mixed, dried wild mushrooms ½ pint (300ml) water	Soak the mushrooms in water for 30 minutes. Reserve for later.
1¾ pints (1 litre) strong *Vegetable Stock* (see page 127) or strong *Poultry Stock* (see page 128) if not a veggie	Bring the stock to simmering point, and keep it there, for the duration of the cooking.
1 lb (450g) field mushrooms 1 medium-sized onion 1 glass white wine 6 oz (175g) Italian risotto rice (Carnaroli or Arborio) reserved soaked mushrooms and liquor reserved field mushrooms and stalks 1 teaspoon mushroom ketchup	Slice the field mushrooms quite finely and chop up the stalks. Peel the onion and chop finely. Bring the wine to the boil in a large saucepan and cook the onion in it for 5 minutes. Turn the heat down, and stir in the rice with a wooden spoon. As soon as the liquid is absorbed, start adding the hot stock, a ladleful at a time, stirring the rice all the time, making sure that the stock is absorbed before you put in more, and never letting the rice stick. Keep everything at simmering point and stir gently throughout: this will take about 20 minutes, though

halfway through, you can get away with adding 2 ladlefuls at a time.

When you have used up most of the stock, stir in the wild mushrooms and their liquid, the field mushrooms and ketchup.

Let the risotto cook on gently for a few minutes until the mushrooms have softened, shrunk and released their moisture. Put in the remaining stock.

---

2 oz (50g) of half-fat Cheddar cheese, grated

3 oz (75g) Parmesan cheese, finely grated

2 tablespoons finely chopped fresh parsley

pepper

shavings of truffle, if using, or 1 teaspoon truffle sauce

Remove from the heat and stir in the Cheddar, two thirds of the Parmesan, the parsley and pepper. Mix in the truffle sauce or shave over some truffle.

Stand for 5 minutes before serving with the remaining Parmesan.

NOTE:

This is a dish that can be reheated in the microwave on a medium setting with success, as microwaving moisturises. Very useful sometimes.

Emily's Pasta

My seventeen-year-old daughter, Emily, who has been a stalwart and adventurous consumer of the recipes in this book, also rather likes to cook, from time to time. This is her best dish, or anyway the one she likes to eat most, as do we all.

Cook quickly and lightly: you do not want the sauce to be a mush but to be *al dente*, like the pasta (see photograph).

SERVES 4–6

2 medium-sized onions	Peel the onions and chop finely.
2 garlic cloves (optional)	Peel the garlic, if using, and cut into slices.
6 plum tomatoes	Skin the tomatoes and chop each one carefully into 8
1 dessertspoon olive oil	pieces.
	In a heavy-based saucepan with a lid, heat the oil and cook the onion and garlic gently for 5 minutes.
	Add the tomatoes and their juice and cook for another 5 minutes.

½ pint (300ml) tomato juice – more if required	Add the tomato juice and wine and simmer gently for a few minutes.
1 glass of red wine	Then add all the flavourings and seasonings and stir around.
1 tablespoon mushroom ketchup	Take off the heat, cover the pan, and keep warm.
several shakes of Worcestershire sauce	
a few drops of Tabasco (optional)	
1 teaspoon Slite or sugar	
salt and pepper	
grated nutmeg	

Mozzarella Wheels
page 26

Duck and Apricot Parfait

page 27

Tomato Jelly
with Quails' Eggs
page 29

Dark Green Astringent Salad

page 36

Fragrant Spinach Soup

page 49

Emily's Pasta
page 64

Pipérade Peppers
page 67

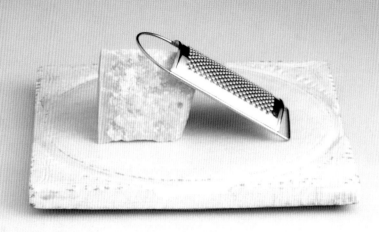

Broccoli and Cauliflower Mustard-Cheese
page 60

Emily was very small when the family moved into Number Eleven and spent a lot of her time at Number Ten with the policemen who guarded Downing Street

salt	In a very large pan, bring plenty of salted water to the boil.
1 lb 2 oz (500g) fresh tricolour pasta	Add the pasta and cook according to the instructions on the pack, or for a minute less than they say.
3 tablespoons roughly shredded basil leaves	Drain well. Put into a large serving dish and pour over the sauce.
pepper	Stir in the basil leaves and grind over lots of pepper.

small chunks of lean ham (optional)	If using any of the optional extras, scatter them over the top of the dish.
small slices of Peperami (optional)	Grate a little Parmesan over the pasta at the table.
a few cooked prawns (optional)	
Parmesan cheese, to taste	

Clara's Macaroni Cheese

S o-called because Clara Barby, Emily's great friend and almost one of the family, once said she liked it, poor child: she gets it every time. It's become famous because the many teenage visitors to the house, asked what they'd like for their supper in front of the inevitable video, now say 'Clara's Macaroni Cheese'. So do Nigel and Tom, when poorly or in need of comfort after a disappointing cricket match or something on Sky Sports. Even Emily's school once asked for the recipe. It could not be easier and makes use of reduced-fat products.

SERVES 4

9 oz (250g) dried macaroni (wholemeal if you think they will wear it) 1 teaspoon salt	Preheat the oven to 200°C (400°F, Gas 6, Aga top oven). In a large pan, boil plenty of salted water. Add the macaroni and cook according to the instructions on the pack. When cooked, strain in a colander and pour boiling water through to get rid of any residual starch. Finally, pat with kitchen paper and transfer to a shallow ovenproof dish.
1 pint (600ml) *Light Cheese Sauce* (see page 130) 2 tablespoons mustard powder 2 Peperami sticks, chopped (optional) 4 oz (100g) lean ham chunks (optional) 2 oz (50g) soya 'bacon' bits (optional)	Meanwhile make the cheese sauce, then stir in the mustard powder. Pour the sauce over the macaroni and mix it in with any optional ingredients you are using.

1 tablespoon Parmesan cheese, grated	Grate over the Parmesan and add the pepper.
pepper	Bake in the preheated oven for 30 minutes or until brown and crispy on top. Remove from the oven and leave to stand for 10 minutes before serving.

Pipérade Peppers

Pipérade is a classic Basque dish and very attractive piled, unconventionally, into peppers of whatever colour you feel like (see photograph). It is idiosyncratic to serve it with wild rice, which I love, but its addition makes this a substantial, meatless and economical meal.

SERVES 4

2 large red peppers	Preheat the oven to 230°C (450°F, Gas 8, Aga top oven).
2 large yellow peppers	Put the peppers in a large bowl in the sink and pour boiling water over them.
	Leave to stand for 5 minutes, then drain and refresh them under cold running water.
	Slice off their tops and reserve. Scoop out the pith and seeds, taking care to keep the pepper cases intact.
	Pat them dry inside and out with kitchen paper.
	Place the peppers upside down on a baking tray and cook in the oven for 15–20 minutes, until softened.
	Put them on a serving dish, open end up, and keep warm.
4 oz (110g) wild rice	Cook the rice in water with the vegetable stock added,
1 vegetable stock cube or powder	according to the instructions on the pack. When cooked, drain and keep warm.

2 garlic cloves (optional)
8 shallots or 3 medium-sized onions, weighing about 8 oz (225g)
1 lb (450g) ripe plum tomatoes
the reserved pepper tops

Meanwhile peel the garlic, if using, and chop finely.

Peel the shallots or onions and chop finely.

Skin and finely chop the tomatoes, and chop the good bits of the reserved pepper tops.

---

4 large eggs
salt and pepper
1 tablespoon extra virgin olive oil

Whisk the eggs in a bowl with salt and pepper to taste. Set aside.

Heat the oil in a large, non-stick frying pan over a medium heat.

Cook the shallots or onions, garlic, if using, and chopped pepper for 10 minutes, or until softened but not brown.

Add the tomatoes and cook, stirring everything around, for a further 5 minutes.

---

2 tablespoons finely-chopped fresh parsley
more pepper

Turn the heat up to high, then pour the beaten eggs into the pan of vegetables. Scramble until done to your liking.

Add the parsley and extra pepper and spoon the mixture into the peppers quickly, to avoid the eggs hardening too much.

To serve, arrange the rice and any extra egg mixture around the stuffed peppers.

Home-Made Hamburgers

There are times when another delicately arranged, pastel and green, 'light' dish is not what the pit of the stomach is crying for. This could be brought on when you pass McDonald's or after the cinema. Try home-made hamburgers instead.

SERVES 4

1 medium-sized onion, peeled	Chop the onion roughly and work in a processor until quite fine.
1 slice bread (any)	Tear up the bread into pieces and add, with the parsley, to
3 tablespoons fresh parsley	the machine – process again until you have achieved large, seasoned breadcrumbs.

1 large plum tomato	Skin the tomato and chop finely; put it in a large bowl with
1 lb 2 oz (500g) lean minced beef, maximum 5% fat (or mince your own from a piece of rump)	the minced beef.
	Add the cheese, breadcrumb mixture, Worcestershire sauce, Tabasco, if using, and salt and pepper.
2 tablespoons grated half-fat Cheddar cheese	
1 teaspoon Worcestershire sauce	
a shake of Tabasco (optional)	
salt and pepper	

1 egg, beaten	Add the egg and mix everything with your fingers (or a plastic spatula, if you must).

Then form into 8 little patties and put them on a board in
the fridge until you are ready to cook them.

When raring to go, heat a non-stick pan over a medium
heat, put in the burgers (4 at a time, if necessary) and
cook for 4–7 minutes on each side, depending on how
you like them.

4 wholemeal muffins, split and toasted	Serve a burger on each half of the wholemeal muffins; there will be 2 per person, but with no lids. Serve the burgers with a little raw tomato relish, made with 2 or 3 peeled and finely-chopped tomatoes, 1 shallot, garlic and a teaspoon of ready-made pesto: simply com- bine those ingredients in a bowl.

Nigel's Scrambled Eggs

O ur lovely dog, Tigger – a tricolour Cavalier King Charles
spaniel – was dragged out every Budget Day along with the
children and me to the dreaded early morning photocall in St
James's Park (see photograph). I also habitually walked him very early
in the morning there. I am not a natural early riser, not by any manner
of means, but at Downing Street I was obliged to get up earlier and earlier because of the sheer amount to get through every day and because,
anyway, Nigel rose at 6am every morning throughout his Chancellorship
and often met his colleagues at 8am, at Number Eleven. It was tricky
to loaf around in a dressing gown.

My feelings of feebleness were exacerbated by the fact that, however
early I got up, I never once caught Margaret Thatcher with her bedroom curtains closed – her bedroom window was at right angles to our
flat and easily visible. The worst thing was that she was also always still
up, lights on, when I went to bed wearily at night. She clearly had the

Tom had to have the day off school to attend the dreaded early morning 'photocalls' in St James's Park which were de rigueur *each Budget Day*

most remarkable metabolism. Everyone started early in that street. Frequently as I returned from the dog walk, at 7 or 7.30am, I'd bump into Bernard Ingham or Charles Powell, hurrying purposefully to their desks at Number Ten.

Poor Tigger became seriously ill and we had trouble getting any food down him. One morning I made both him and Nigel some soft scrambled eggs. Tigger didn't eat his, but Nigel did, and complained that it was far too peppery. This was a mystery, since I hadn't used any pepper. The embarrassing fact was that he'd eaten Tigger's, into which I'd crushed a Vetzyme dog-vitamin tablet, in hope. So now you know what Vetzyme tastes like. Luckily, Nigel suffered no ill effects – but, sadly, Tigger died.

In those days, our eggs were scrambled with a hefty knob of butter and milk. Nowadays, I do them in the microwave. Provided you watch like a hawk and whisk them out of the microwave the instant they are setting, in order to fork them up like mad, this produces an excellent version. You need no butter and only a tablespoon of water. Furthermore, the microwave bowl is easier to clean than an eggy saucepan.

SERVES I

2 eggs	Whisk the eggs in a bowl that is suitable for a microwave
salt and pepper	oven.
1 tablespoon water	Add a little salt and pepper. (Be careful to avoid crushed
	Vetzyme.)
	Stir in the water.
	Microwave for 2 minutes. Inspect. Carry on microwaving
	until the eggs start to set, then remove from the oven
	and fork briskly until they look right.

Fishy Dishes

In some moods, my feelings about fish come out as a passionate diatribe. It is so disappointing that we, inhabitants of an island, have to go so far in our shopping trips to obtain fish of quality. The reasons are many, including, it has to be said, some very dodgy political ones.

Fish is, however, low in fat and a very good source of protein: ideal food for dieters as good fish does not need to be dressed to kill. Adornments are what usually add calories.

Some of the farmed fish that have become so cheap a source of protein have also lost their fishy-ness. And what is put into their feed and environment to kill off parasites doesn't bear thinking about. All I can say is that if you have a good, reliable place to buy fish, use it to capacity. For the rest of us, there are swift postal services from decent sources that offer a good but – inevitably – expensive alternative.

SERVES 6 AS A FIRST COURSE

12 oz (350g) smoked salmon trimmings 5 tablespoons virtually fat-free fromage frais or quark the juice of a lemon pepper	Cut the smoked salmon into small pieces with scissors. Process until very smooth with the fromage frais, lemon juice and pepper.
4 fl oz (120ml) *Fish Stock* (see page 127 or use half a stock cube, if necessary, dissolved in water) ¹/₂ sachet of powdered gelatine (or the whole sachet if doing in one big mould)	Bring the stock to the boil, let it cool a little, then add the gelatine and stir until completely dissolved. Leave the jelly mixture until cool, but not set, and then add to the mousse, stirring in well. Turn into 6 ramekin dishes or mould. Refrigerate until set. If you have used a mould, turn out the mousse by putting a serving dish on top of it and inverting sharply. You may need to de-fridge it slightly before embarking on this process.
6 slices bread, toasted 1 lemon, cut into wedges	Cut each slice of toast into 4 fingers. Serve the mousse with fingers of hot toast and lemon wedges.

Saffron Scallops

This is the prettiest of delicate dishes (see photograph). It is not at all difficult to make: just be aware that overcooked scallops become tough and disappointing and lose their special sweet flavour. Save a bit of time for the final stage, which involves patient and steady arranging skills.

SERVES 4

2 large, well-flavoured tomatoes	Preheat the oven to 180°C (350°F, Gas 4, Aga baking oven). Skin and core the tomatoes. Cut the firm flesh into very
salt and pepper	neat and small cubes. Add salt, pepper and chives.
1 tablespoon snipped chives	Reserve 24 tomato cubes and a scattering of chives for final decoration.
12 scallops, preferably in their shells	Separate the scallops' whites and corals. Put in an ovenproof dish, lined with enough foil to make a
1 tablespoon lemon juice	parcel, with the lemon juice, wine and shallot. Loosely close the foil.
2 tablespoons dry white wine	Bake in the oven for 15–20 minutes, until the scallop whites lose their translucency, but be careful not to overcook them.
1 shallot, very finely chopped	Remove the corals and as much shallot as you can fish out. Keep the whites warm, still loosely wrapped in their foil.
a few threads of saffron	Put the saffron in a small bowl, pour over the hot juices from the foil parcel and leave for a few minutes to steep.
1 egg yolk, beaten	Chop up the corals carefully and mix with the tomato
4 tablespoons half-fat crème fraîche or low-fat yoghurt	mixture. Set aside. Heat the saffron juices to bubbling in a small pan. Take off the heat and stir in the egg yolk and then the crème fraîche or yoghurt. Return to a very gentle heat, season, and stir into a smooth sauce with a wooden spoon.

the reserved tomato cubes	Keep warm (but do not cook further) while you arrange the scallops: carefully slice each white scallop body in half across and arrange around the edge of an individual plate. Put a little of the coral and tomato mixture in the middle of each plate. Pour the sauce over the white scallops. Top each serving with a little of the reserved tomato cubes and the reserved chives.
the reserved snipped chives	

Steaming Mussels

I think of this as a greedy person's treat: the bowl of mussels looks so wonderfully plentiful (see photograph) but as you spend so much time extracting the little mouthfuls of moules, because most of the bulk is the shells, you won't in fact overeat. (The same is true of whole globe artichokes: it amounts to a spot of harmless self-delusion for dieting purposes.)

Good mussels grown on ropes are quite easy to buy, and remarkably cheap. If I were in the restaurant business, I'd use them a lot. Don't be fobbed off with tiny ones, though – they are not worth the trouble.

SERVES 4

4½ lb (2kg) of mussels 1 dessertspoon porridge oats	Fill the sink with water and scrub the mussels with a firm brush. Pick off their beards. It is a long and horrid job but you must do it. If any of the mussels are open, throw them away – it means they are dead and certainly 'off'. Rinse all the good ones again in cold, running water.
	Transfer to a very large bowl, cover generously with cold water, add the porridge oats and leave in a cool place for a couple of hours: the mussels eat the oats and this somehow gets rid of any grit and sand in the shells.

6 shallots

2 garlic cloves

3 plum tomatoes

$1/2$ pint (300ml) dry white
wine

a generous shake of
Tabasco

the juice of a lemon

Peel the shallots and garlic and chop finely.

Skin the tomatoes and chop into cubes. Drain and rinse
the mussels and put them, with the shallots, garlic,
tomatoes, wine, Tabasco and lemon juice, into a very
large pan that has a lid. I use my big wok.

Bring to the boil. Put on the lid, lower the heat, and steam-
cook for 5 minutes, shaking the pan from time to time.

Halfway through, turn everything about with a slotted
spoon.

4 tablespoons finely
chopped parsley

pepper

a baguette

If any mussels haven't opened during cooking, discard
them. Add the parsley and pepper. You don't need salt
with these creatures from the sea.

Divide between large individual bowls, ensuring everyone
has plenty of the soup, or serve in a big tureen.

Serve with bread for dunking and mopping up the delicious
juices.

Trout Baked in a Parcel

This is the simplest possible way to cook fish and less smelly and messy than many other methods. It is readily transferable to any firm-fleshed species but it is particularly appropriate if you have to settle for farmed trout, which most of us do: it badly needs flavour-enhancing tricks.

SERVES 4

1 fennel bulb 1 medium-sized 'old' carrot	Preheat the oven to 180°C (350°F, Gas 4, Aga baking oven). Trim the fennel and chop roughly for the processor. Chop the carrot into similar-sized pieces. Pulse-process the vegetables into small bits.
4 whole trout, gutted and wiped out 1 lemon, cut into 8 wedges, pips removed 4 shallots 4 tablespoons dry white wine salt and pepper	Lay each trout on a piece of foil, big enough to make a parcel. Fill their tummies with the carrot and fennel mix. Pop two wedges of lemon in each one. Slice the shallots into rings and spread on top of the trout. Pour 1 tablespoon of wine over each fish. Sprinkle over the salt and pepper. Wrap the parcels up fairly tightly and stand for an hour if possible in a cool place, on a baking tray. Cook in the oven for 25 minutes. Remove fish carefully from the foil and serve. *Lemon Sauce* (see recipe on page 131) is very nice with the trout.
NOTE:	Keep the bones, juices and skins of the fish to make stock.

Constituency duties were a good excuse for fish and chips – Nigel, Thérèse and Emily in Stoney Stanton, Leicestershire, during the 1987 General Election campaign

Flashy Fish

One of the specialities of the French Riviera, also found in Spain, is fish – usually sea bass, *bar* or *loup de mer* in Provence – baked in a flamboyant salt crust. *Le beau monde* that tends to congregate in that beautiful area expects fabulous food, and I have eaten very well indeed there, courtesy of the French Socialist Government – *inter alia* – while Nigel was in that line of business.

So long as you can lay your hands on, and pay for, an excellent fish, this is an exciting way to present it. You could probably do it just as well in ordinary foil but it would not look the same and the salt crust certainly keeps in the moisture of the fish very effectively. It is essential to buy a fish that will speak for itself and does not need disguising with a heavy sauce. Curiously, the fish does not emerge too salty – I suppose because you remove the crust all in one before serving – but you will not need to add extra salt on the plate.

SERVES 4

3 large eggs 1 box (9 oz/250g) coarse 　sea salt crystals 1 tablespoon flour	Preheat the oven to 200°C (400°F, Gas 6, Aga baking oven). Separate the eggs (reserve the yolks for a sauce or to make 　yolky-yellow scrambled eggs). Mix the whites with all the salt in a large bowl and add the 　flour to help make the mixture sticky.
1 whole, gutted sea bass 　or John Dory, 　weighing 2¹/₂ lb 　(1.15kg) 2 sticks lemon grass ¹/₂ a lemon pepper	Wipe over and inside the fish with kitchen paper. Put it in a suitably-sized roasting pan. Top and tail the lemon grass, crush lightly, and cut into 　small lengths. Insert into the cavity of the fish along with the lemon, cut 　into 4 wedges. Grind pepper over the fish. Then, using your hands, spread the salt mix over the fish to 　cover it completely, as if using pastry. Bake in the oven for 25 minutes.
2 lemons, cut into 　wedges	Serve on a fish plate with lots of lemon wedges and make a 　fuss about breaking off the hard salt crust, which you 　have to discard, along with the lemon and lemon grass 　inside the fish. Remove backbone and fillet the fish into 　portions.

Oriental-Style Fish-Rice

It is helpful to use a wok with a lid for this dish. Because of its bowl-shaped base, you can put in only a little oil. You have to have the food in smallish bits and toss it about constantly to stir-fry and cook rapidly – all aids to less absorption of fat. If you don't have a wok, a deep casserole pot or even a large frying pan with a lid will do.

If very fresh fish is unavailable, the frozen skinned blocks of fish in supermarkets are of good quality and convenient to use. And it is much more likely that the fish won't have hung around at all. If you do need to skin the fish yourself, it's easy if you have it very cold or not fully defrosted: nick the skin at the wider end of the fillet and then, holding the blunt edge of the knife firmly between the skin and the flesh to steady the fish, pull off the skin firmly and all in one piece.

For extra flavour, cook the rice in fish stock if you have it. For this recipe, prepare all ingredients before you start as the final cooking is more or less instant.

SERVES 4

4 good-sized pieces of firm white fish (cod is ideal), weighing about 7–8 oz (200–225g) each, skinned	If using frozen fish, defrost and drain well. Cut the fish into large chunks. Cook the rice in salted water, according to the instructions on the pack. Drain thoroughly, fluff up and keep warm.
8 oz (225g) rice (a mixture of Basmati and wild rice is my favourite for this dish)	
salt	

4 shallots
1 garlic clove (optional)
1/2 fennel bulb
1–4 green chillies (4
    makes a *very* spicy
    dish)
2 sticks lemon grass

Meanwhile, prepare all the vegetables and spices: peel and
    finely chop the shallots and garlic, chop the fennel into
    small cubes, de-seed and slice the chillies. Top and tail
    the lemon grass and leave whole.

1 dessertspoon oil
    (safflower or other
    light oil of choice)
4 small tomatoes
1 glass vermouth or the
    juice of a lemon

Heat the oil in the wok to just smoking.
Add the prepared vegetables and spices and stir-fry until
    softened – 5 minutes or so.
Skin the tomatoes and chop finely.
Add them to the wok, then add the vermouth or lemon
    juice.
When everything is bubbling, put in the fish chunks, put on
    the lid and turn the heat down to minimum. Steam-cook
    in this way for 10 minutes, or until the fish has turned
    opaque.

1/4 pint (150ml) canned
    coconut milk
2 tablespoons chopped
    fresh coriander leaves

Turn up the heat again and when the food is simmering,
    add the coconut milk and stir in gently.
Take the wok off the heat, add the rice and coriander and
    mix it in.
Pick out the lemon grass sticks, with tongs.
Serve in small Chinese-type bowls, ensuring that everyone
    has a good mix of fish, juices and rice. There should be
    more than enough for thirds.

Red Hot Kedgeree

You can prepare everything in advance for this dish as you cook all its components separately first – it takes just a few moments to put together at the end.

How spicy you have it is simply a matter of taste: I've suggested minimum and maximum amounts of pep. I expect in Imperial India, whence the dish originated, it was fairly hot. Classic 'khichri', if there is such a thing, is usually cooked with lots of butter and cream. It is sensational but disallowed on the diet. Sorry.

According to Elizabeth David's *Spices, Salt and Aromatics in the English Kitchen*, the original dish contained no fish but did include red lentils, as well as rice. I have compromised by using Camargue red rice and our own traditional smoked haddock. It is a mix that works.

Best cooked in a wok or heavy-based casserole with a lid.

SERVES 2–4 FOR BREAKFAST, LUNCH OR SUPPER

5 oz (150g) Camargue red rice 1¼ pints (725ml) *Fish Stock* (see page 127 or use a cube if you haven't got stock in the freezer)	Put the rice in a sieve and rinse with cold water. Bring the rice to the boil in ¾ pint (450ml) of the stock, stir, cover and simmer for 30 minutes. Reserve the rest of the stock. Leave the rice to stand in the stock until ready to cook the kedgeree.
1 egg	Hardboil the egg, steep in cold water and peel carefully when cool enough to handle. Chop into small, neat pieces.

12 oz (350g) smoked haddock fillets – about 3 – fresh or frozen, and undyed	Skin the fish. For an easy way to do this, see the description in *Oriental-Style Fish-Rice*, page 83. Put the haddock in a frying pan. Add enough water to half cover the fish and then poach for 7–8 minutes until almost cooked. The fish gets cooked a bit more later. Drain and cut into large chunks.
1 medium-sized red onion 1 clove garlic 1–2 small red chillies $\frac{1}{2}$ teaspoon butter or *ghee* 1 teaspoon sunflower or safflower oil 1 teaspoon turmeric powder 1–3 teaspoons garam masala (depending on your spiciness threshold)	Peel the onion and garlic and chop very finely. Chop and de-seed the chillies (use 2 chillies if you like your food spicy). Heat the butter or *ghee* and oil in the wok or casserole and quickly stir-fry the onion, garlic and chillies. Put in the spices, stirring constantly. Add the rice: there is no need to drain it unless you want a very dry sort of kedgeree.
the reserved fish stock $2\frac{1}{2}$ oz (60g) of 0% fat Greek-style yoghurt	For the final stage, add the fish to the pan with the reserved stock, using as much as you like: some like their kedgeree moist and others prefer it drier. Add the chopped egg towards the end – if you put it in too soon, it will go leathery – and as soon as everything starts to bubble, take off the heat. Carefully stir in the yoghurt and put on the lid. The kedgeree keeps warm pretty happily (on a sideboard hotplate for breakfast in the days of the Raj, I bet), but rarely hangs around for long in our household.

Salmon in Avgolemono

It is not easy to find here the dense, white fish from the Mediterranean Sea that the Greeks typically use when cooking this dish. Unless you have a good source of very fresh fish, you might prefer to use farmed salmon – which is both readily available and reasonably priced nowadays, but, I am afraid, lacks flavour. Preparing it in this aromatic broth, however, imparts enough taste to make it very acceptable.

Avgolemono is a delicious, comforting and filling family meal – and is cooked all together in one large pot on top of the stove. It keeps warm relatively well, too.

For this recipe you need a very large, heavy-based saucepan or stew-pan with a lid – mine holds 8½ pints/5.7 litres.

SERVES 4

1 large leek	Top, tail and slice the leek, carrot and celery into thick
1 large carrot	discs.
1 head (about 6 sticks) of	Cut the lemon half into 4 pieces.
celery	Put the prepared vegetables and lemon in the saucepan
½ a lemon	with the wine, salt and pepper. Boil for 5 minutes.
¼ pint (150ml) dry white	Add the water.
wine	Bring to the boil, put on the lid and simmer very gently for
salt and pepper	30 minutes. Don't overcook the broth or it will turn sour.
2 pints (1.2 litres) water	Using a slotted spoon, take out and discard the lemon
	pieces.
	Remove about half of the vegetables and process them with
	a little of the broth to a mush. Return to the pan.

8 oz (225g) new potatoes, scrubbed or peeled, or 4 oz (110g) long grain rice, rinsed in cold water to get rid of excess starch	Get the broth simmering again, add the potatoes or rice, and simmer for 10 minutes.
2 lb (900g) salmon in one piece, cut from the middle (or use a piece of good white fish of choice)	Add the fish and courgettes to the pan.
	Continue cooking with the lid on for 15 minutes or until the fish is just cooked – pierce with a knife down the backbone to check that the flesh has just turned opaque, but do be careful not to overcook.
10 baby courgettes, weighing about 12 oz (350g) rinsed	Remove the fish from the pan and keep warm.
1 yellow courgette, weighing about 8 oz (225g), rinsed and cut into thick discs	
2 eggs	Beat together the eggs and lemon juice in a separate bowl.
the juice of 2 lemons	Add a ladleful of hot broth to the egg and lemon and whisk together.
	Then remove the pan from the heat, add the egg and lemon sauce (the avgolemono) and whisk it in, rotating the pot to amalgamate everything.
	Cover the soup and vegetables to keep them warm while you skin the fish, remove its backbone, and cut into portions.
	Put into a large serving dish or tureen.
	Ladle the soup and vegetables over the fish, and serve in bowls that will hold plenty of soup as well as the fish and vegetables.

Mackerel with Gooseberry Cheese

Mackerel is one fish that is not difficult to find fresh, and it remains cheap, so far. Make sure it is absolutely fresh, though. It should be shiny, slippery, firm and bendy. Mackerel is nutritious: it contains Omega-3 fatty acid which is said to be very good for your heart. It is chock-full of flavour.

If you cook it in the oven, as in this recipe, the kitchen will not retain lingering fish smells for too long.

Gooseberries are a classic accompaniment to mackerel for a very good reason: their sharpness cuts through the oiliness. If fresh gooseberries are available, of course use them. Stew 9 oz (250 g) of gooseberries with 4 teaspoons of Slite and 3 tablespoons of water until softened (about 15 minutes). Leave to cool and then use as below. Canned gooseberries are acceptable, however, in this recipe: any sweetness retained from the syrup used in the canning process is offset by the savoury fromage frais.

SERVES 4

4 mackerel, each weighing about 12 oz (350g), gutted and with heads and tails removed	Preheat the oven to 200°C (400°F, Gas 6, Aga baking oven).
	Wipe the fish inside and out with kitchen paper.
	Cut one of the lemons into 8 wedges and insert 2 into the cavity of each mackerel.
2 lemons	Squeeze the juice from the other lemon. Sprinkle the lemon juice over the fish.
salt and pepper	Season with salt and pepper.
	Wrap each fish in a loose parcel of foil, put on a baking tray, and cook in the preheated oven for 25–30 minutes, or until done. Test by piercing the fish down the backbone with a knife – the flesh should have turned opaque.

9 oz (250g) of gooseberries, prepared with Slite, as described above, or a 10 oz (275g) can of gooseberries, drained thoroughly	Meanwhile prepare the gooseberry cheese: combine the gooseberries, fromage frais and pepper in a processor, or push the gooseberries through a plastic sieve and mix in the other ingredients.
2 loaded tablespoons virtually fat-free fromage frais	When the mackerel is ready, carefully remove the backbone and put the fillets into a warm serving dish. Remove the skin if you prefer to.
pepper, to taste	To serve, heat the gooseberry cheese very gently in a saucepan to just below boiling, and spoon it over the mackerel fillets.

Prawns, Scallops and Bacon with Chestnut Mushrooms

This makes a fabulous 'composite' meal: if you have one, cook and serve it in a wok. Otherwise a large, lidded casserole pot suitable for the hob and table is fine. The bacon is legitimate because nothing else in the dish is fatty and it is okay to have bacon now and again, for Heaven's sake!

The flavours of scallops (sweetish) and bacon (salty) seem to set each other off very well. And the final dish, if you use red rice, emerges as a pleasing deep mottled brick colour.

SERVES 4

3 oz (75g) Camargue red rice	Bring the rice to the boil in lightly salted water, cover with a lid, and cook gently for about 30 minutes. The texture is meant to be nutty.
salt	Drain very well and set aside.

8 large scallops (in their shells, for preference)	Meanwhile, prepare all the other ingredients. Pick over the shellfish. Defrost and drain thoroughly, if necessary.
8 oz (225g) large raw (grey) prawns, peeled (only use cooked prawns if you have to)	If using raw prawns, put them in a Pyrex jug in the sink. Pour boiling water over them and leave to stand for a few minutes until they have turned pink. Drain, pat dry with kitchen paper and set aside.
8 oz (225g) chestnut mushrooms	Clean the mushrooms with kitchen paper. Separate the stalks from the mushrooms. Leave the cups of the mushrooms whole, but slice the stalks thinly.
7 oz (200g) lean bacon, snipped into strips with scissors (or use soya 'bacon' chips) the juice of half a lemon 2 fl oz (55ml) dry white wine 1 teaspoon mushroom ketchup	Put the bacon in the bottom of the wok or casserole. Add the mushroom cups and stalks. Stir-fry briskly over a medium heat. As soon as the mushrooms are beginning to soften, put in the lemon juice, wine and mushroom ketchup. Stir in the scallops and put on the lid. Steam-cook for 5-10 minutes or until the scallops have just cooked and look white, not translucent. Don't overdo them or they will be tough.
a 14 oz (400g) can of haricots verts 2 oz (50g) fresh rocket leaves 1¹/₂ oz (40g) fresh parsley, finely chopped pepper	Put in the prawns. Drain the haricots verts well and add to the pan with the rocket leaves, parsley and pepper. Finally, stir in the rice. Take off the heat and put on the lid for a few minutes to keep warm. If the prawns and scallops look too big, slice them appropriately. Serve when you are ready. This dish is nicest lukewarm.

Proper Dinners

One good meal a day is a reasonable expectation even on a diet. Recipes in this section incorporate ideas for adapting familiar dishes into less fattening versions that should leave no one feeling deprived of a proper dinner.

I certainly thought of it as a proper dinner the first time Nigel invited Denis and Margaret Thatcher to dine with us at Number Eleven. The occasion was intended to bend the Prime Minister's ear in private before the presentation of Nigel's first Budget to the Cabinet and then the House of Commons. The dinner *à quatre* subsequently became an annual pre-Budget event.

Shortly before each time, the Treasury team took over Chevening – the Foreign Secretary's official residence in Kent – for a weekend of Budget decisions and a frolicking evening after their hard day's work. (I have not forgotten the game of charades in which Peter Rees, then Chief Secretary to the Treasury, starred in the rôle of Geoffrey and Elspeth Howe's dog, named Budget: Peter's leg-lifting skills were top-class.)

As we all left on Sunday, there was an opportunity to buy pheasants that had been shot on the estate over the weekend. So I came back to London that first time with two fully-feathered braces, to prepare for the Prime Minister's dinner. Fortunately, the Number Eleven doorman, Arthur Woolley, had been a butcher in the Co-op in an earlier incarnation. Although the Co-op had never required him to pluck a pheasant, we decided it would be no worse than tackling a chicken. I recall a very feathery kitchen, however, halfway through.

Arthur was a wonderful asset: another odd thing that happens to Government Ministers is that twice a year they receive venison from the Royal Parks. The more important the Minister, the larger the

Our Number Eleven household – from left to right: Arthur Woolley, the Chancellor's doorman who doubled as Master Butcher of Royal Game (see page 93); Nanny Extraordinaire, Joy Reid; Marie Collier, the Chancellor's Messenger; and Mary Montgomery, my other pair of hands

amount of venison, so by the time we occupied Number Eleven, it was half an animal that arrived – in one piece and delivered in a sack. Arthur, though, simply thought of it as a small cow and managed to dissect the huge lump into manageable portions.

The dinner for Margaret Thatcher went very well in the end. I cooked the Chevening pheasants in Normandy fashion with an apple and onion sauce, Calvados and loads of cream. Nowadays, I use instead the self-thickening sauce technique and low-fat yoghurt (see, for example, the recipe for *Boozy Pork with Apple* on page 110): it is just as good. Margaret was absolutely charming and I became very fond of her, but the children's abiding memory of the evening is of poor Tom, then about seven years old, standing in front of the sitting room fireplace in his dressing gown, being advised by the PM on the importance of

The neighbours were generous in allowing us to use their garden – Margaret Thatcher, Emily, Tigger and a television crew

learning his times-tables by heart: he'd been rash enough to mention his trouble with sums.

Emily introduced the dog, Tigger (see *Nigel's Scrambled Eggs* on page 70), who was thereafter permitted to use Number Ten's garden. This made early morning life in Downing Street much more tolerable – see photograph above of the PM, Emily and Tigger.

Poussin Parcels

This simple and delicious dish allows the dieter to have a bit of pastry. I think of it as a substitute for *Chicken Kiev* which, loaded with breadcrumbs and garlic butter as it must be, is too fattening. One poussin will be ample for two people, as the filo pastry and filling bulk up the portions (see photograph).

When essential greasing arises, as in this case for the skin of the bird, you will use less if you dip your fingers into a little dish of oil and rub it all over with your fingertips. This trick is also excellent nutrition for your cuticles.

SERVES 2

---

1 poussin
1 teaspoon or less of
  olive oil
¼ of a lemon
	Preheat the oven to 190°C (375°F, Gas 5, bottom shelf of
	  the Aga top oven).
	Using your fingertips, smear the skin of the poussin with a
	  little of the olive oil and stuff it with the lemon.
	Roast in the preheated oven for 30–40 minutes, or until the
	  juices run clear when the thickest part of a leg is pierced
	  with a skewer.
	Rest for 5–10 minutes, then carefully carve off the breasts
	  and remove the skin.
	Turn the oven down to 170°C (325°F, Gas 3, Aga baking
	  oven).

---

2 tablespoons light
  fromage frais
2 tablespoons finely
  chopped fresh basil,
  tarragon or parsley
	Put the fromage frais in a small bowl and stir in the herbs,
	  garlic, if using, and salt and pepper to taste. Spread
	  liberally over each poussin breast.

Saffron Scallops

page 77

Steaming Mussels

page 78

Fillet of Beef with Sauce Poivrade and Spring Greens in a Wok

pages 104 and 117

Poussin Parcels and Green Sauce

pages 96 and 132

Boiled Ham with Slimmers' Parsley Sauce

pages 109 and 130

Elderflower Jelly
page 141

Purple Hearts
page 145

Quirky-Quarky Soufflés

page 150

2 garlic cloves, very finely chopped or crushed (optional)

salt and pepper

4 sheets filo pastry

Grease your fingers again and prepare for the parcels: place two sheets of filo across each other in the shape of a cross for each parcel. Work quickly with filo as it gets brittle if left for long in the air. Put a poussin breast on the double-thickness middle bit, bring up the ends of both sheets, and gently twist, to close the little packages.

Smear a baking tray all over with olive oil, arrange the parcels on it, and bake for 10–15 minutes, until golden brown.

Green Sauce (see page 132), to serve

Remove carefully from the baking tray and serve with the green sauce.

NOTE:

To make the base for *Chicken and Fennel Soup* (see recipe on page 48): carve the meat from the legs and thighs of the poussin, cut into strips and reserve. Put the remainder of the carcass and skin into a pan with a well-fitting lid, add a couple of carrots, celery if you have it, and an onion, roughly chopped, cover with cold water and bring to the boil. Cover and simmer for several hours.

Lemon-Stuffed Roast Chicken

When I was a child, roast chicken was a rare and big treat. We had it only when one of my grandfather's birds popped it. Now there is a certain snobbery about chicken, just because it has become cheap and available, I suppose, to the extent that it's considered mean to serve it at dinner parties. This is absurd. A good chicken is full of protein, low in fat, extremely good value-for-money and simply delicious, especially when plainly roasted and served with well-flavoured gravy.

SERVES 4

1 lemon	Preheat the oven to 220°C (425°F, Gas 7, Aga top oven).
a fresh chicken, weighing about 2¹/₂–3 lb (1.15–1.35kgs), giblets removed	Cut the lemon into quarters. Remove the pips and stuff the lemon quarters into the chicken. Tuck in all the flaps of skin and put the chicken on a rack in a roasting pan.
1 teaspoon ready-made fresh pesto	Spread the pesto over the breasts and legs of the bird.
pepper, to taste	Grind over the pepper.
8 leaves of basil	Tuck the basil leaves into the crevices of the chicken. Roast for 30 minutes in the preheated oven.
the juice of another lemon	Take the chicken out of the oven and pour the lemon juice over it.
Granny's Gravy (see recipe on page 128), to serve	Turn the oven down to 180°C (350°F, Gas 4, Aga baking oven) and cook for a further 1–1¹/₂ hours until done. To test, pierce the thickest part of a leg with a skewer – the chicken is cooked if the juices run clear.
	Rest the chicken for 15 minutes in a warm place to allow the juices to permeate while you prepare the gravy and vegetables.

Do not forget to remove the lemon quarters from inside the
bird before carving.
Serve with the gravy.

Pheasant, Beetroot and Turnip with Black Potatoes

ame is relatively unfatty and pheasant is readily available frozen, if you haven't access to fresh birds. It is also much cheaper than it used to be. If you do have to use frozen birds, which inevitably lack the full flavour of well-hung, fresh specimens, be sure to defrost them slowly and drain them well of any liquid, before starting to cook.

Plain-roasted, pheasants can be dull and dry. You certainly won't experience these problems if you cook them this way: the sauce comes out a lovely terracotta colour, not beetroot red. And I really do think that there is a natural affinity between beetroot and game. Turnips too are a delicious root vegetable, in my opinion but not everybody's, and go very well with this dish.

The recipe works equally well with partridge – a glorious bird, but for most of us, not so easy to find.

SERVES 6

8 small beetroot, weighing about 1 lb (450g)	Boil the beetroot whole in plenty of water until tender – about 40 minutes.
2 medium-sized onions	Plunge into cold water, top and tail, and peel – easy, but
³/₄ pint (450ml) *Poultry Stock* (see page 128), degreased	wear disposable gloves if you are concerned about getting pink fingers. Peel the onions and chop each one into 8 pieces.

Process half the beetroot (reserving the rest), all the raw onion and chicken stock, to a coarse consistency – not smooth like a soup. Set aside.

---

2 pheasants
1 teaspoon allspice
    berries
1 tablespoon safflower or
    sunflower oil
1 glass red wine
6 baby turnips, peeled
    and cored like an
    apple

Preheat the oven to 180°C (350°F, Gas 4, Aga baking oven).
Wipe the pheasants inside and out with kitchen paper.
Crush the allspice berries in a pestle and mortar. Heat the oil in a large, heavy-based casserole with a lid and fry them briefly in the oil over a medium heat.
Then put in the pheasants and quickly sear on all sides.
Pour over the wine and let it bubble for a couple of minutes.
Put in the beetroot, onion and stock mixture, and the turnips.
Bring back to simmering point, cover the pan tightly with foil and put on the lid.
Transfer to the oven and cook for 45 minutes or until the birds are done. To test, pierce the thickest part of a leg with a skewer – the pheasant is cooked when the juices run clear.

---

the reserved beetroot
7oz (200g) tub half-fat
    crème fraîche or 0%
    fat Greek-style
    yoghurt
2 tablespoons finely
    chopped fresh parsley
salt and pepper

Remove the pheasants and carve. Nigel always slices the meat off the legs to make a more elegant presentation.
Discard all the skin and yellow fat.
Keep the flesh warm (and keep the bones to make an excellent stock).
Put the reserved beetroot (cut in half if they look too big) into the sauce and heat through.
Return the pheasant slices to the casserole to keep hot.
Remove the beetroot and turnips with a slotted spoon and place in a large serving dish. Place the pheasant on top.
Remove the sauce from the heat and carefully stir in the crème fraîche or yoghurt.
Season to taste, pour the sauce over the meat and sprinkle the parsley over the dish.

NOTE: *Black Baked Potatoes* go well with this dish, not least
because they soak up the sauce and therefore need no
butter. Choose the variety carefully for the purpose and,
to bake to perfection, pierce 3 large potatoes several
times over with a skewer and microwave them on high
for 8 minutes, or until a little soft when squeezed gently.
Then put in a preheated 220°C (425°F, Gas 7, Aga top
oven) for about 30 minutes, until blackened. Allow half
a large potato per person

Lilac Duck Breasts

Duck has very fatty skin – one reason for the flesh being so suc-
culent and full of flavour – and could easily be something a
dieter felt compelled to forego. That would be sad, so we do
eat it from time to time but cooked in such a way as to minimise the
amount of fat. One of the reasons duck is so often served with orange
is because the fruit cuts through the fat. I prefer to use tart purple fruits
with duck – with the pink of the duck breasts, the resulting dish is of
lovely lilac colours.

SERVES 4

4 duck breasts   Preheat the oven to 220°C (425°F, Gas 7, Aga hot oven).
Prick the skin of the duck all over with a skewer, which will
allow some of the fat to escape during cooking.
Place the duck breasts on a rack in a roasting pan and cook
in the preheated oven – 20 minutes for pink flesh, 25
minutes for better done. They will continue to cook a bit
while resting, so, if anything, underdo the time.
As soon as the duck is cool enough to handle, strip off the

skin – quite easy if you start at one corner and pull purposefully. Pat the breasts with kitchen paper to absorb more fat and rest in a warm place.

1 tablespoon duck dripping 1 tablespoon flour 1 tablespoon crème de cassis ¼ pint (150ml) boiling water	Discard all the fat in the roasting pan except for a tablespoonful. Place the pan over a medium heat, reheat and quickly add the flour, then gradually add the cassis, and water, stirring constantly. Simmer until a thickened, smooth sauce forms.
4½ oz (125g) blueberries or blackcurrants, picked over	Now add the fruits and simmer gently in the sauce until softened – 5–10 minutes. Transfer the sauce to a processor and work until the berries are well mixed in. Reheat gently. Carve the duck breasts into delicate slices and arrange on the serving plates. Pour over a little sauce, but serve most of it separately at the table. Delicious with peas and new potatoes.

Surf and Turf Fondue

You need a fondue set with special forks to serve this dish properly and to have guests who won't balk at DIY. I find it especially popular with teenagers.

The first time I sampled fondue done in this way was in Davos, Switzerland, where the family had ventured for a skiing holiday organised by the Lords & Commons Skiing Club. It was a fateful trip: son Tom broke his shoulder on his first outing and Nigel, who was seriously overweight, kept falling over and suffered the embarrassment of having to ask for help to become upright. I think this was a motivating factor in his slimming resolution: it was the year preceding the start of his diet. The fondue was the only consolation.

SERVES 6

1 piece of fillet steak, weighing about 6 oz (175g)	Cut the fillet of beef and the chicken breasts into mouthful-sized strips.
2 skinless and boneless chicken breasts	Peel the prawns. Wipe the mushrooms.
12 large raw (grey) prawns	Put each of the ingredients in separate bowls on a lazy Susan or in a divided dish.
6 oz (175g) button mushrooms	

1 dessertspoon Worcestershire sauce	Sprinkle Worcestershire sauce over the steak and chicken, lemon juice over the prawns, and a little salt and pepper over the mushrooms.
the juice of half a lemon	
salt and pepper	

5oz (150g) 0% fat Greek-style yoghurt	Make a dip by softening the yoghurt with the dessertspoon of lemon juice and stirring in the chives and cucumber.
1 dessertspoon lemon juice	Season.
4 tablespoons snipped fresh chives	
a 1-inch (2.5cm) piece cucumber, peeled and finely diced	
salt and pepper	

3 x 14 oz (400g) cans consommé (with sherry, if available)	Heat the consommé gently to simmering point. Put the baguette in a very low oven to warm through. Transfer the consommé to the lit fondue set.

THE NIGEL LAWSON DIET COOKBOOK

1 baguette	Put 6 of the prawns into the consommé to give everyone a head start; slice the bread, and summon the cooks to the table.
	Put out bowls as well as small plates so that at the end, you can serve everyone with a bowl of soup from the fondue pot, which will have a lovely, strong flavour from all the bits that have been cooked in it.
	The bread is for dunking in the soup.

Fillet of Beef with Sauce Poivrade

This is a family favourite and we have it when I'm feeling flush (see photograph).

SERVES 6

a piece of fillet beef, weighing about 2–2$\frac{1}{2}$ lb (900g–1.15kg)	Marinate the beef in a non-metallic dish with the Worcestershire and soy sauces at room temperature for an hour or two. Reserve the juices.
1 tablespoon Worcestershire sauce	Preheat the oven to 220°C (425°F, Gas 7, Aga top oven).
1 tablespoon soy sauce	Place the meat on a rack in a roasting pan and cook in the preheated oven for 10 minutes. Turn the oven down to 180°C (350°F, Gas 4, Aga baking oven) and cook for another 20 minutes for the Bleu Brigade but 30 minutes is probably about right for Pinks. You really have to judge this for yourself.
2 tablespoons brandy	Warm the brandy in a separate pan, pour it over the fillet and take a match to it to flame. This is a potentially

4 shallots, peeled and
   very finely chopped
1–2 tablespoons soft
   green peppercorns,
   drained and crushed in
   the pestle and mortar
   (2 tablespoons makes
   it pretty spicy)
salt
4–5 tablespoons half-fat
   crème fraîche
1 tablespoon finely
   chopped fresh parsley

dangerous operation: do it off the heat but while still very hot.

Remove the fillet from the pan and rest in a warm place (the meat, not you!) for 10 minutes.

To make the sauce, reheat all the juices in the pan, add the shallots, and peppercorns to taste. Simmer for 5 minutes. Add salt, to taste.

Take the pan off the heat, stir in the crème fraîche and parsley and keep warm.

To serve, slice the beef thinly or into 6 steaks, whichever you prefer.

Pour the sauce, well stirred at the last minute, over the beef. *Spring Greens in a Wok* (see recipe on page 117) go very well with this dish.

Hot Pot Beef

This is another favourite beef dish and we have it when I am *not* feeling flush. It is cooked in a most unfattening way, is full of flavour and the beef is always wonderfully tender.

SERVES 6

a joint of rolled brisket,
   weighing 2¹/₂–3 lb
   (1.15–1.35kg)
1 tablespoon mushroom
   ketchup
1 tablespoon soy sauce
1 tablespoon sesame oil
2 garlic cloves, peeled
   and sliced (optional)

Marinate the beef in a non-metallic dish with the ketchup, soy sauce, sesame oil and garlic, if using, at room temperature for an hour or two.

Turn the joint over halfway through so that both sides absorb the flavours.

3 medium-sized onions, peeled	Preheat the oven to 140°C (275°F, Gas 1, Aga baking or simmer oven).
4 large carrots, rinsed	Cut the onions in half across their diameter.
2 turnips, peeled	Chop the carrots, turnips and celery into 4 or 5 pieces each.
1 head of celery (4–5 sticks), trimmed	

4 oz (110g) field mushrooms, sliced thickly	Heat an ovenproof casserole with a lid.
	Put in the beef and juices and let it sizzle for a few minutes either side to brown.
¹/₂ pint (300ml) hot, strong stock	Add the root vegetables, mushrooms, hot stock and a good grinding of pepper.
black pepper	

1 oz (25g) fresh parsley, finely chopped	Cover the casserole tightly with foil and then put on the lid. Bring to the boil, allow to bubble for a few minutes and transfer to the oven.
salt (optional)	
	Cook for 4 hours or more: the precise time doesn't matter, though within reason, the longer the beef cooks, provided it is at a low temperature, the more tender it will become. If you have an Aga, cook in the baking oven for the first 30 minutes, then transfer to the simmer oven where you could easily leave it overnight or all day.
	When ready, remove the joint from the casserole.
	Remove about a third of the vegetables with a slotted spoon and work them to a mush in a processor.
	Return the vegetables to the pot and stir well to achieve a thickened gravy.
	Add half the parsley, and put the casserole on the hob over a medium heat to keep everything hot while you carve the meat into slices and arrange in the serving dish.
	Pour the gravy and lovely chunks of vegetables over the meat and sprinkle with the remaining parsley. Only add salt if necessary.

Serve with copious quantities of spring greens or other
cabbage that has been lightly cooked and seasoned.
Grated nutmeg is good with greens. Dumplings are off.

French Roast Leg of Lamb with Ginger

L amb, like most other meat, of course carries fat but it would be a
serious deprivation to eliminate it from your repertoire. Cook it
with lots of flavouring but no added fat. This method, which can
be adapted to other joints of meat, ensures succulence and is truly delicious. The pre-lunch aromas make it irresistible.

SERVES 6—8

1 leg of lamb, weighing about 3 lb (1.35kg) a 3-inch (7cm) piece of fresh root ginger 1 garlic clove (optional)	Preheat the oven to 220°C (425°F, Gas 7, Aga top oven). Put the lamb in a non-metallic dish. Peel and chop the ginger and garlic, if using, into slices. Spread around and under the joint.
1 tablespoon Worcestershire sauce several shakes of Tabasco 1/2 pint (300ml) red wine	Mix together the Worcestershire sauce, Tabasco and red wine and pour over the joint.
several sprigs of fresh rosemary	Tuck the rosemary in around the joint. Let it all stand, covered with a cloth, for a couple of hours at room temperature. Turn it over after an hour.

¼–½ pint (150–300ml)
hot, strong stock

Put the lamb and marinade in a roasting pan without a rack and cook in the preheated oven for 30 minutes.

Turn the oven down to 170°C (325°F, Gas 3, Aga baking oven).

Carefully remove the pan from the oven, pour the stock over the joint, cover the pan loosely with foil, and return to the oven for 1½ hours or until the meat is done to your preference. Test it with a skewer to see what colour the juices are or, if you still aren't sure, carve off and nibble a slice from the outside, which will enable you to judge what the inside is like. The usual rule of thumb for lamb is 25 minutes to the pound for pink meat, but we like ours quite French, and cook it for a bit less.

When ready, remove the joint from the pan and let it rest for 10–15 minutes on the carving board in a warm place.

Strain and skim the fat from the juices left in the pan. A plastic 'gravy separator' jug is useful for this purpose. Reheat the juices in a saucepan, stirring well, and use as your gravy, adding extra stock if there isn't enough.

Do not give the dieters the outside slices with skin. Save them for the children who need some fat for the health of their hair and much else.

Serve with roast celeriac and lots of other vegetables.

Boiled Ham with Slimmers' Parsley Sauce

Although versions of hot ham with glazed honey topping and similar are delicious, this homely version is less fattening.

SERVES 4–6

1 unsmoked gammon joint (middle-cut is thought to be the best), weighing 2¹/₂–3 lb (1.15–1.35kg) 1 small potato, peeled water, to cover	Put the gammon joint and potato in a large saucepan with a lid, cover with water and bring to the boil for a few minutes. The potato is meant to absorb excessive saltiness but this may be what Emily calls an 'old mothers' tale'. Drain and discard the water and potato to get rid of the scum and brine.
³/₄ pint (450ml) dry cider	Return the joint to the pan, pour in the cider and top up with water to cover generously.
2 medium-sized onions, peeled 1 large 'old' carrot 10 black peppercorns	Chop the onions and carrot into 8 pieces and add to the pan, with the peppercorns. Bring to the boil, cover, and simmer for about 1³/₄–2 hours, calculating 30 minutes to the pound plus 30 minutes over.
Slimmers' Parsley Sauce (see page 130)	Turn off the heat and leave the joint standing in its liquid for at least 15 minutes, while you prepare your sauce and vegetables (broad beans, mangetout and new potatoes are especially good with hot ham – see photograph). When ready to serve, drain thoroughly, strip off the rind and fat, and carve thinly.

Boozy Pork with Apple

P ork crackling is undoubtedly one of life's fattening pleasures: you have to judge for yourself how often to indulge. No reason anyway for not enjoying pork itself. Pork can sometimes emerge a bit stringy, especially if not cooked in a lot of fat. This recipe guarantees tender meat and a delicious sauce.

SERVES 4

1 medium-sized Bramley apple, peeled	Preheat the oven to 200°C (400°F, Gas 6, Aga top oven).
1 medium-sized onion	Reserve a third of the apple, rub it with a cut-up lemon to prevent it discolouring, and cut the rest into chunks.
1 large 'old' carrot	Peel the onion and chop roughly.
¹/₂ a lemon	Top and tail the carrot and slice into 8 pieces.
1 piece of boned and rolled pork shoulder, loin or leg weighing about 21/2 lb (1.15kg)	Heat a heavy, ovenproof casserole with a lid over a medium heat. Sear the joint on all sides.
	Add the prepared vegetables and apple, stirring quickly to prevent them from sticking.
¹/₂ pint (300ml) dry cider	Pour over the cider and the water. Bring to the boil, and
¹/₄ pint (150ml) water	then simmer for a couple of minutes.
salt and pepper	Add salt and pepper and cover tightly with foil, put on the lid and transfer to the preheated oven.
	After 30 minutes, turn the oven down to 150°C (300°F, Gas 2, Aga simmer oven).
	Leave to cook for 2 hours or more. This is a matter of judgement and you need to know your oven. With pork, it is important that it is thoroughly cooked, and within reason it doesn't matter if it is left in a low oven for longer than specified.

the reserved apple
salt and pepper
a 5 oz (150g) tub low-fat
    yoghurt

When ready, carefully remove the joint from the casserole and keep it warm.

Remove the solids from the pot, using a slotted spoon; place in the processor and work until quite smooth. Stir into the liquid left in the casserole, then reheat gently.

Peel and grate or chop very finely the rest of the apple and add to the pot.

Taste and season again, if necessary.

Remove from the heat and stir in the yoghurt.

Carve the meat and serve with the sauce poured over or handed separately. Sprouts with boiled chestnuts go particularly well with this dish.

Easter Turkey

Turkey is an excellent source of low-fat protein and has become very good value for money. It can, however, come out dry. Roasting it in stock ensures moist flesh and also avoids the need for smearing the bird with lots of fattening butter or covering with bacon strips.

SERVES 8

a 6–7 lb (2.7–3.2kg)
    turkey
1 dessertspoon sesame oil
a 1-inch (2.5cm) piece of
    root ginger, peeled

Preheat the oven to 220°C (425°F, Gas 7, Aga top oven).

Smear the turkey's breasts and legs with the oil, using your fingers.

Grate the ginger all over: a rotary Parmesan grater is excellent for the purpose.

Put the turkey in a large roasting pan without a rack.

Roast in the preheated oven for 30 minutes.

1 pint (600ml) strong
  Poultry Stock (see
  page 128)
1 glass of red wine

Turn the oven down to 170°C (325°F, Gas 3, Aga low
  baking oven).
Heat the stock to boiling point.
Remove the pan from the oven, turn the turkey upside
  down, pour the wine and then the stock over the turkey.
Cover the pan loosely with foil and return to the oven.
Cook slowly for around 2¹/₂ hours; halfway through this
  cooking time, turn the bird the right way up.
Remove the pan from the oven and pour off most of the
  stock, keeping it for gravy. Turn up the oven to the
  original temperature.
Return the turkey to the oven for 30 minutes or more until
  fully cooked and the skin is crisp and golden brown.
Test the bird by piercing the thickest part of the leg with a
  skewer – the turkey is cooked if the juices run clear.
When done, leave it to rest in a warm place for 15
  minutes before carving.

Monday Curry (and Stock)

Use a wok, if you have one, or a large casserole.
  When you have leftover chicken or turkey, you don't have to
have it cold with mayonnaise, good though that can be. A
spicy curry instead has the added advantage, I don't know why, of
helping to clear your head after overdoing it: perhaps it's to do with
your system getting so busy dealing with the spices that it is obliged to
forget its other woes.

First, carve off the good meat from the turkey and dice it into nice-
looking, substantial chunks. Set aside for the curry. Then break up the
carcass to make stock. (Put it in a saucepan with a lid and cover
with water. Add a roughly chopped onion, a large carrot and any other

casserole vegetables you have. Bring to the boil, add salt and pepper, and skim. Simmer very gently with the lid on for 2–3 hours. Strain, skim again, cool and freeze for future use.)

SERVES 4

1 large onion	Peel and finely chop the onion and apple.
1 apple	Heat the oil in a wok or large casserole.
1 dessertspoon safflower or sunflower oil	Add the onion and apple and stir-fry for a couple of minutes.
1 small chilli, green or red, chopped very finely and de-seeded	Add the chilli and garlic, if using.
1 garlic clove, peeled and sliced finely (optional)	Put in the star anise, poultry, korma sauce, coconut milk and garam masala.
4–8 star anise (depending on your spiciness threshold)	Stir it all around and simmer gently for 10 minutes, trying not to break up the bits of meat.
the leftover poultry, weighing about 1 lb (450g)	
1 standard-sized can korma sauce (approximately 14 fl oz/400ml)	
1/4 pint (150ml) canned coconut milk	
1–4 teaspoons garam masala (again depending on your spiciness threshold)	
a 2 1/2-inch (6cm) piece of cucumber	To make a raita for your curry, put the yoghurt in a small serving bowl.

1 shallot a 5oz (150g) tub very low-fat yoghurt pepper	Dice the cucumber and peel and finely dice the shallot. Stir into the yoghurt and grind the pepper over the top.

1 teaspoon desiccated
    coconut (optional)
Basmati rice (allow 1½
    oz/40g dry weight per
    person), cooked
	Turn the curry out into the serving dish and sprinkle with a
	    little desiccated coconut, if you have it.
	Serve with Basmati rice and the bowl of raita, a cooling
	    accompaniment for curries.

Vegetable Variety

Vegetables play a very valuable role in this eating plan. It is now accepted that a healthy diet should incorporate plenty of vegetables and, for dieters who are cutting down on starch, the fibre that vegetables provide becomes even more important.

A crafty slimmer-cook will gradually increase the amount of vegetables served with a meal to compensate for slightly decreased portions of meat. Shifting the balance, even by a little each time, can make quite a difference overall in terms of calories.

Vegetables also lend themselves to virtuous cooking methods, notably steaming, but also stir-frying, dry-roasting and baking. Truly delicious are spring greens, purple sprouting broccoli, Brussel tops, spinach, chards and other deeply coloured leaves, fresh and roughly shredded to be steamed simply with a little salt.

A main meal based on vegetables (for examples, see *Luncheon Mushrooms* on page 58, *Baked Butternut Squash* on page 121, or *Pipérade Peppers* on page 67) is perfectly satisfying and if you are having it instead of a meat, fish or cheese-based meal, the chances are that you have 'at a stroke' reduced your intake of fattening food.

Courgettes and Goats' Cheese (v)

Goats' cheese is a little less fattening than many others and, as it has a very strong flavour, you do not need to use a lot to know you've had cheese, which dieters do need to be careful with, yet often crave.

Courgettes are often ruined by cooking for too long and in too much water, which makes them unappetisingly squishy. In this recipe, they are just blanched and then baked for a few minutes, so that they remain firm and full of flavour.

This is a lovely starter, or you could have it as a savoury – or even as buffet 'finger' food. It is very easy to make.

SERVES 4

4 large courgettes	Preheat the oven to 200°C (400°F, Gas 6, Aga top oven). Put the courgettes into a large bowl and cover with boiling water. Leave to stand for 10 minutes. Remove the courgettes and wipe dry. Top, tail and cut in half lengthways. Carefully scoop out the seedy middles of the courgettes, so you have a groove down the middle of each. Cut each courgette half into 4 pieces.
5 oz (150g) medium-fat, soft goats' cheese pepper	Melt the cheese, either in the microwave on low for a few minutes or in a bowl over a saucepan of boiling water. Pick out the rind, if you don't fancy it, but I don't think there is anything wrong in eating it. Spoon the cheese into the grooves of each courgette piece. Grind over the pepper. Put on a baking tray and cook for 10–15 minutes in the oven, or until the cheese is just beginning to bubble.

Spring Greens in a Wok

Judy Ridley (widow of Nicholas – of whom I was very fond, greatly admired and miss) is a very close friend of mine and also an excellent cook. The trout and salmon that Nick and Judy used to fish themselves and cook to share with their friends were exquisite. She once said to me that it would be a great help if we could solve the problem of producing a dinner – we were both involved in the 'happening' political scene at that point – with vegetables that had to be kept warm and got soggy while we were doing our best to be perky and polite in the drawing room.

It is even more tricky if you are entertaining alone, of course. I have often puzzled over the problem and do not think there is a perfect solution. However, vegetables cooked in the wok go halfway to solve it because you can do them in stages. Instead of the soy sauce, you could substitute a splash of wine, lemon juice and/or a little water. When ready to serve (if you have an attractive wok, it will double as the serving dish), reheat on a very high heat for a minute if your vegetables are still a bit too crunchy – see photograph.

SERVES 4

1 medium-sized onion	Chop the onion finely.
1 teaspoon sesame oil	Heat the oil in a large wok.
	Stir-fry the onion in the oil for 5 minutes.
1½–2 lb (700g–900g) spring greens, stalks cut off, rinsed and shredded	Add the greens and soy sauce and toss everything together. Put the lid on and leave to steam on a fairly gentle heat, until done to how you like your vegetables.
1 tablespoon soy sauce	Stir in the pine kernels.
1 tablespoon pine kernels	

Three-Times Peas with Baby Onions

This easy-peasy way to cook peas makes a change and the green component of the meal more appealing for reluctant vegetable eaters. It looks quite party-ish.

SERVES 4

2 bunches of spring onions	Cut off the green bits from the spring onions. Peel the white bulbs and slice them thinly.
8 oz (225g) sugar snap peas	Top and tail the sugar snaps and mangetout.
8 oz (225g) mangetout	Cook the podded peas in salt and water until done to your preference. Drain and keep warm in a serving dish.
8 oz (225g) podded fresh peas (or use frozen)	Put the onions and sugar snaps in another saucepan with salt and as little water as you can get away with. Bring
salt	to the boil and cook for 2 minutes, then add the
water	mangetout and cook for a further 2 minutes (or longer if you like your vegetables softer – take one out and test for doneness).
	Drain very thoroughly and add to the shelled peas.
4 oz (110g) prepared *lardons* or lean bacon, cut into strips (optional)	If you're not strictly reducing or vegetarian, the addition of *lardons* or lean bacon, baked until crisp in a hot oven (15 minutes) and drained of as much fat as possible with kitchen paper, is very nice with this dish.

Sesame-Roast Root Vegetables Ⓥ

For information and thought:

JERUSALEM ARTICHOKE: 18 calories per 100g

SWEDE: 21 calories per 100g

BEETROOT: 28 calories per 100g

TURNIP: 36 calories per 100g

CARROT: 42 calories per 100g

CELERIAC: 44 calories per 100g

PARSNIP: 74 calories per 100g

POTATO: 86 calories per 100g

Sesame-roast is a lovely way to have vegetables with a traditional Sunday joint and is considerably less fattening than doing them the usual way in the fat from the meat. Do one, two, or several varieties, depending on how you feel.

You need just over a tablespoon of sesame oil, a shake of flour, and a small amount of sesame seeds, if you like.

---

vegetables of choice,
   allow 4–6 oz
   (110–175g) per person
1 teaspoon lemon juice
salt

Peel the vegetable(s) you have chosen, where necessary. Cut into even-sized pieces, allowing at least 4 bits per person. As a guide, a celeriac of medium size will yield 16 pieces.

Put into a large bowl of cold water and sprinkle a little lemon juice over to stop them going brown.

Drain and boil in fresh, salted water until they yield slightly to the point of a knife, but are still firm.

Drain again and allow to dry off. Pat dry with kitchen paper.

---

4 teaspoons sesame oil	Put the oil in a saucer.
1 dessertspoon flour	Roll each piece of vegetable in the oil, then in the flour and
a tablespoon of sesame	sesame seeds (if using).
seeds (optional)	Cook in a roasting pan in the preheated oven for about 30
	minutes, or until browned and crisped to your liking.

Mashed Celeriac

Only recently have I read in my newly acquired edition of Elizabeth David's *French Provincial Cooking* – the old one fell to pieces – that she, the guru-ess, has a recipe for cooking celeriac unpeeled, and then pulling off the skin afterwards. What a bonus that could be: raw celeriac requires quite some strength to handle and I wish I'd learned this earlier.

Mashed celeriac is delicious with game or meat dishes that include lots of gravy.

SERVES 6

8 oz (225g) potatoes	Peel and chop the potatoes roughly.
1 medium-sized celeriac,	Cut the thick skin off the celeriac and chop into pieces the
weighing about 1 lb	same size as the potatoes (or use Elizabeth David's
(450g)	recently learned method).
salt	Boil the vegetables in plenty of salted water until cooked.
	Drain well.
2 garlic cloves, peeled	Put the vegetables in the processor with the garlic and
(optional)	crème fraîche.
3 tablespoons half-fat	Whizz to a purée-like consistency.
crème fraîche	
salt and pepper	Add pepper, nutmeg and more salt if required, and serve.
grated nutmeg	

Baked Butternut Squash with Hot Courgette Sauce (V)

The children and Nigel don't like squash, they think, and courgettes, pumpkins, patty pans are all categorised by them as no-nos. I think this is because even the word 'squash' implies a soggy, water-sodden mush, which is indeed a fairly disgusting idea. However when we have been on safari in Africa – my favourite holiday – where squash are a staple of the diet, I noticed that there was less resistance. This is because in Africa squash are not just boiled to softness: they are made into fabulous, sweet soups and used as a base for many other delicious dishes.

This recipe for baked butternut squash is as unlike squashed swede as you can get – more like a sweet, baked potato. You can even eat the skin.

SERVES 4

2 butternut squash	Preheat the oven to 190°C (375°F, Gas 5, Aga baking oven).
¹/₂ teaspoon walnut oil	Rinse and dry the squash.
2 teaspoons lemon juice	Cut in half lengthways (this requires a sharp knife, a steady
pepper and salt	pair of hands, and quite a lot of strength). Scoop out the
	seedy bits from the middle of the squashes and discard.
	Grease a roasting pan with walnut oil using your fingers so
	as to spread it evenly and use as little as you can get
	away with.
	Lay the 4 squash halves in the tray, cut sides up and top to
	tail. Put half a teaspoon of the lemon juice in each
	squash's cup. Grind pepper over, and sprinkle on a little
	salt.
	Cover with foil and bake in the preheated oven for 45
	minutes, or until the flesh is soft enough to yield easily
	to the point of a knife.

1 oz (25g) fresh parsley	Meanwhile, make the stuffing:
1 oz (25g) walnut pieces	Rinse the parsley, cut off the stalks and put in the processor
8 spring onions	with the walnut pieces.
1 tablespoon Parmesan cheese	Trim the spring onions and put the white parts in the processor.
another dessertspoon walnut oil	Work everything together until the walnuts have turned into tiny bits.
1 dessertspoon dry sherry	Turn out into a bowl.
salt and pepper	Grate the Parmesan and stir it into the mixture with the oil and sherry to make a paste.
	Season to taste.

1 further teaspoon walnut oil	Turn up the oven to 220°C (425°F, Gas 7, top shelf of the Aga top oven).
1 teaspoon lemon juice	Remove the squash from the oven and remove the foil.
	Put an equal amount of stuffing in each squash cup.
	Sprinkle walnut oil and lemon all over the exposed squash flesh.
	Bake for 20 minutes.

1 large courgette	To make the *Hot Courgette Sauce*, rinse, top and tail the courgette and chop roughly.
	Put the courgette pieces in a bowl and cover with boiling water. Leave to stand for 10 minutes.
	Drain well.

salt and pepper	Process the courgette with salt, pepper and yoghurt, until smooth.
2 tablespoons very low-fat yoghurt	Turn into a saucepan.
	Stirring all the time, heat gently to just under simmering point on top of the stove.

Puréed Peas or Carrots

M y favourite vegetable purées are of carrots or frozen peas, not least because these everyday vegetables otherwise seem too ordinary to put forward. Use low-fat quark rather than butter. Have with very lean lamb cutlets or, perhaps, a piece of fish with a lemony sauce.

You will need 4 small heart-shaped moulds with loose bottoms, or little pots of a similar size.

SERVES 4

8 oz (225g) carrots or frozen petit pois 1/2 teaspoon salt 1/2 teaspoon Slite	If using carrots, top, tail, peel and cut them up into chunks. Bring the peas or carrots to boil in a little water with salt and Slite. If using carrots, cook until just soft. Drain.
1 dessertspoon quark	Work the vegetable to a purée in the processor with the quark. Turn into moulds, and smooth the top. Put in a steamer, bring to the boil and steam for 10 minutes with the lid on. Using a cloth to save your hands from burning, turn out carefully onto plates for serving.

Savoury Sauces, Stocks and Dressings

Thinking he might have to go without sauces while dieting was one of the most disheartening prospects for Nigel: he adores them. That was why I tried to think of ways to make sauces that avoided loads of butter or oil, for those are the calorie-challenging ingredients in classic sauces like hollandaise and mayonnaise. Certainly *Lemon Sauce* (see recipe on page 131) is infinitely less fattening than the hollandaise it is intended to replace, and very delicious. It is versatile too: you can add all sorts of different flavours to it.

Other tricks I have employed include making the maximum possible use of reduced-fat products, as in *Cheese Sauce* (see page 130); *Slimmers' Parsley Sauce* (see page 130) has more parsley than flour in it to achieve bulk; and the 'self-thickening' technique (see below) is seriously useful for dieters. Sauces made from fruits or vegetables are very helpful perks, too.

As for stocks, I am not going to pretend that I'm not a great admirer of stock cubes, powders and the expensive but brilliant tubs of stock that you can buy. I don't think it matters much if there is a trace of monosodium glutamate in a serving of gravy. Having said that, my own freezer is chock-full of polythene tubs containing exotic stocks because I am incapable of wasting carcasses, bones or vegetable off-cuts and, as

I cook such a lot, there is almost always one stock or another simmering away in the Aga. The house constantly smells of broth, which isn't very elegant. I have given easy recipes for basic stocks, in case there are other parsimonious souls like me around.

When it comes to using oils for dressing salads and so on, a good trick is to choose a highly flavoured oil of which you need to use less to get a good taste than you would with a blander version. It is much nicer, anyway, to have the flavour of an appropriate oil predominate.

Self-Thickening Casserole Sauces

The trick here, a small but useful aid to staying slim, is to avoid the usual way of thickening a casserole or stew, which involves *beurre manié* or some other combination of fat and flour. Instead, simply extract some or all of the vegetables you have used in the stew towards the end of the cooking time and process them to a thick mush with a little of the cooking liquid. Return the vegetable mush to the dish and mix in well: you will now have a thickened gravy, without extra fat or flour.

A crucial point is always to include more vegetables than you're used to using in casseroles – about a third more – and a little less meat. Fiddling with the proportions like this is a contribution to a less fatty diet and the result on the plate doesn't appear piously overloaded with vegetables, because the extra veg has been used to make the sauce.

Typical examples of this technique arise in *Hot Pot Beef* (see recipe on page 105) and *Boozy Pork with Apple* (see recipe on page 110).

Stocks

Vegetable Stock (v) is the most basic, useful for any vegetarian recipe, and to build on for other uses. The ingredients, or acceptable approximations, are almost always there in the average refrigerator.

MAKES ABOUT 2½ PINTS (1.5 LITRES)

1 onion 2 carrots 1 leek 1 fennel bulb or 3 celery sticks	Rinse and chop all the vegetables roughly. There is no need to peel them.

¼–½ pint (150–300ml)
   dry white wine
water, to cover, up to 2½
   pints (1.5 litres)
1 lemon, cut into 4
the stalks from a bunch
   of parsley
black peppercorns, about
   a dozen
salt
	Put the vegetables and wine into a large saucepan with a lid and boil for a few minutes.
	Add the water, lemon, parsley stalks, peppercorns and salt. Bring to the boil again, and then boil fiercely for at least 30 minutes, or simmer with the lid on for 1½ hours. Strain.

Fish Stock is one to have stored in the freezer as in practical terms you will make it only after you have cooked some fish, and will not necessarily want to use the resulting stock the next day. You might also find it useful to add flavour to sauces, so it is a good idea to freeze the stock in cubes in an ice tray and then decant the cubes into polythene bags for keeping frozen.

To make *Fish Stock*, omit the lemon but otherwise proceed as for *Vegetable Stock*. Put enough water in the pan to well and truly cover the bones and trimmings (but not the livery bits) from any fish that you have had. Skim it thoroughly, twice if necessary, before sieving carefully and storing. And don't cook it for any longer than 45 minutes or it could become sour.

For *Poultry Stock*, break up the carcasses of whatever birds you have cooked and follow the same procedure as for *Fish Stock*. Again, omit the lemon – and you don't really need the wine. Sip it instead, perhaps. You need to simmer the stock for up to 1½ hours, lid on, once it has come to the boil.

NOTE: For **strong stocks**, return the sieved stock to the pan and boil fiercely, with the lid off, until reduced to about half the original quantity.

Granny's Gravy

My sisters and I all make good gravy, we think. It is a relic of our childhood: our mother was past-master at it and we children smothered our food in gravy, as the amount of meat we could have was strictly limited, due to post-war economy.

This is how we do our gravy nowadays, using less of that lovely meat dripping that we used also to get for tea on hot toast. Oh ho: those were the days!

MAKES ABOUT 1½ PINTS (850ML)

1 tablespoon meat juices	Drain off all the fat, leaving behind the juices from under the joint of meat. (It is entirely up to you whether you keep the rest for the toast treat later. Some would say that anything goes in private.)

1 pint (600ml) strong stock (see page 127 or use cubes if you have to)	Heat the stock.
	Heat the roasting pan with the meat juices over a medium heat.
1 tablespoon flour	Add the flour, quickly stirring it into the meat juices with a wooden spoon.
1 glass red wine and/or 1 teaspoon mushroom ketchup or 1 teaspoon Worcestershire sauce or 1 teaspoon Marmite (all optional)	Add the hot stock and stir like mad until the gravy is smooth and bubbling.
	Dilute with more stock or water if necessary – dieters should really have thin gravy – and add wine and/or other flavourings, to taste.
	Reheat to boiling, and strain through a sieve if you fear there are any lumps.

Light White Sauce

This sauce is the base for a number of flavoured sauces, and a perfect accompaniment for certain vegetables in itself. My absolute favourite is very young broad beans cooked in their pods: the flavour is out of this world. Sadly, you very rarely find them for sale – the vegetables are left to grow large enough to produce plump and substantial beans, whose pods are too tough to eat. If by any chance you find them young enough, or grow them yourself, simply boil them rapidly, drain them very well as they tend to retain moisture, and serve with this *Light White Sauce*.

The sauce is also delicious with ordinary fresh broad beans. I think it is worth taking a few minutes before serving to slip off the skins from the cooked beans – the result is less chewy and quite chic.

Another excellent use for *Light White Sauce*, with or without the addition of parsley or chives, is over beetroot that have been boiled in their skins until tender (about 40 minutes) and then quickly peeled.

MAKES ABOUT ¾ PINT (450ML)

1 dessertspoon butter
1 dessertspoon flour
¹/₂ pint (300ml)
    semi-skimmed milk
	Make a roux by melting the butter over a gentle heat and
	    stirring in the flour with a wooden spoon.
	Add the milk, a little at a time, stirring continuously to
	    ensure smoothness.
	Allow the sauce to simmer very gently for 2–3 minutes,
	    until the flour has cooked and the sauce has thickened.
	    If there are any disastrous lumps, you can rescue your
	    sauce by beating it with an electric whisk or working in
	    a blender.

salt, pepper and grated
    nutmeg (optional)
2 tablespoons very
    low-fat fromage frais
¹/₂ oz (25g) fresh chives
    or parsley, snipped
    (optional)
	Add the seasonings, to taste.
	Then remove from heat and stir in the fromage frais.
	Cover the pan and leave the sauce to stand in a warm place
	    for 20–30 minutes, during which time it will thicken
	    further.
	Stir in the herbs according to taste, if using, and reheat
	    gently.

	Use this base for making **Slimmers' Parsley Sauce** too –
	    use ³/₄ pint (450ml) of milk and 'thicken' the sauce with
	    a generous amount of finely-chopped parsley (about
	    6 tablespoons). You may want to omit the fromage frais.

	For a lovely **Light Cheese Sauce** add to the *Light White
	    Sauce* ¹/₄ pint (150ml) of water and 9 oz (250g) of
	    half-fat Cheddar cheese, grated. Flavour with a teaspoon
	    of mustard powder. Don't rush to serve it the moment it
	    is ready: keep it warm, covered with clingwrap to
	    prevent a skin forming, while it expands. Again, the
	    fromage frais is optional.

Lemon Sauce

I t is best to make this sauce well in advance as it takes so long to set. Then either keep it warm, covered with clingwrap or, if you make it the day before, you will find that it reheats satisfactorily in a microwave on a medium setting. Be sure to whisk it again when reheating. This is a seriously useful sauce and can be used instead of mayonnaise or hollandaise, hot or cold.

MAKES ABOUT ½ PINT (300ML)

6–8 fl oz (175–225ml) good quality *Poultry, Fish* or *Vegetable Stock* (see pages 127–8) the juice of a lemon	Preheat the oven to 110°C (225°F, Gas ¼, or use the Aga simmer oven). Heat the stock to boiling and transfer to a medium-sized ovenproof bowl. Add the lemon juice.
2 large eggs	Beat the eggs in another bowl and then whisk them into the liquid with a balloon whisk. Put the sauce, uncovered, into the oven and forget it for 45 minutes or so. Then remove from the oven and give it a whisk. If it isn't yet thick, return to the oven for another half an hour. It is ready when it has a custard-like consistency but you must judge for yourself whether you want it like a frothy mousseline-type sauce or thicker, like a mayonnaise. Whisk again.
NOTE:	You can also make the sauce in a microwave oven, on a low setting. Follow the procedure outlined above, but microwave for ten-minute periods until it reaches the desired thickness, whisking every time you check it. It takes about half an hour altogether, done this way.

To make *Green Sauce*, lightly cook 8 oz (225g) of young spinach (or sorrel if you like that sharp taste – or some and some), drain it very well, squeeze dry in a wad of kitchen paper, and process into a purée. Stir into the lemon sauce and reheat very gently.

Tomato Sauce

Tomato sauce is endlessly useful, both in recipes for pasta or rice dishes and for an addition to treats like hamburgers. It will keep for quite a long time in the fridge if well sealed in a clean and lidded container.

MAKES ABOUT 1 PINT (600ML)

2 medium-sized onions	Peel and chop the onions and garlic.
2 garlic cloves	Place in a heavy saucepan with ¹/₄ pint (150ml) of the
¹/₂ pint (300ml) tomato juice	tomato juice and boil for 5 minutes. Reserve the remaining tomato juice.
4–6 plum tomatoes, weighing about 14 oz (400g)	Skin and chop the tomatoes. Add to the pan, turn down the heat, and simmer for a further 5 minutes.
1 teaspoon Slite	Add all the flavourings and extra liquids.
2 shakes of Tabasco	Stir everything around for a few minutes.
3 shakes of Worcestershire sauce	
2 tablespoons red wine	
the reserved tomato juice	
¹/₄ pint (150ml) of water	

949

1440

Kingston

1 tablespoon pitted black olives	Crush the olives roughly.
	Add the olives and herbs to the sauce; stir until simmering, then remove from the heat.
3 tablespoons finely chopped fresh basil leaves	Leave to stand in a warm place for 15 minutes to allow the flavours to infuse.
2 tablespoons finely chopped fresh parsley	Liquidise to the texture you prefer.

NOTE:	For a coulis, or really smooth sauce, push the tomato sauce through a nylon sieve.

Cranberry and Mandarin Sauce

This is a delightful and colourful, tart sauce for turkey, duck and other poultry and game. It is less fattening than conventional cranberry sauce because you can avoid using the large quantity of sugar that cranberries demand, being so sour. If you use a lot of fruit in proportion to liquid, you can also get away with 'thickening' the sauce without using fat and flour.

You can serve this hot or cold.

SERVES 8

a 10 oz (275g) can mandarin orange segments in natural juice	Drain the mandarins, reserving the juice.
	Place the cranberries, Grand Marnier, and half the juice from the can of mandarins in a saucepan. Bring to the boil, reduce the heat and then simmer until the berries pop open and feel quite soft – 10–15 minutes.
9 oz (250g) cranberries, fresh or frozen	

2 tablespoons Grand Marnier (optional) or 2 extra tablespoons of juice from the canned mandarins	Put in the processor with the orange segments and whizz until well mixed. Return to the saucepan and reheat, adding more fruit juice if the sauce is too thick.
grated nutmeg (optional) Slite to taste or runny honey (optional)	Grate in the nutmeg, if using, and taste for sweetness: if you find the sauce too tart, add Slite or honey until the sauce is less sharp (the amount of sweetener or honey each person will get in their dollop will be fairly minimal and acceptable for dieters). Serve the sauce as it is or strain through a nylon sieve, if you want a smoother-looking sauce.

Nutty-Flavoured Salad Dressing

Everyone has their own favourite salad dressing and if you are attuned to the flavours of oils, you can vary the dressing to taste and fancy. I rarely use vinegar because I find it makes me splutter but, like the oils, there are some fine vinegars around to choose from. Particularly nice in my opinion are raspberry, cider and balsamic vinegars. Sometimes it is obvious that a particular flavour is appropriate – cider vinegar, for instance, with an appley salad.

For my money, freshly squeezed lemon juice with hazelnut oil (or walnut oil, which is, however, less delicate) is a combination that is hard to beat for a refreshing, light dressing for salad leaves. It could not be simpler to prepare.

MAKES ENOUGH TO DRESS A SALAD FOR 4

2 tablespoons hazelnut oil	Put all the ingredients in the base of the salad bowl and stir together.
2 tablespoons lemon juice	Add whatever salad leaves you are using and turn them
¹/₂ teaspoon Slite	around gently in the dressing with your fingers, to
a little salt and pepper, to taste	ensure that all the leaves are covered. Serve straightaway.

Pumpkin Seed Dressing

This dressing is special because the pumpkin seed flavour predominates and goes particularly well with certain salads, including tomato-based dishes, kidney beans and other pulses.

MAKES ENOUGH TO DRESS A SALAD FOR 4

1 tablespoon pumpkin seed oil	Put all the ingredients in a clean jam jar with a tight-fitting lid and shake about to mix well.
2 tablespoons lemon juice	Add the seeds when about to dress the salad and shake
salt and pepper	again.
¹/₂ teaspoon Slite	
a tablespoon of pumpkin seeds	

Yoghurt Dressing

This is very low-fat by comparison to mayonnaise and excellent for leafy salads, to which it adds a sharp tang. For an even sharper dressing, add an additional tablespoon of vinegar; for a more mellow dressing just use the one.

MAKES ENOUGH TO DRESS A SALAD FOR 4

3 tablespoons 0% fat
   strained Greek-style
   yoghurt
2 teaspoons Dijon
   mustard
1–2 tablespoons vinegar
   of choice
1 tablespoon water
1/2 teaspoon garlic
   powder
salt and pepper
1 teaspoon Slite or sugar

Put all the ingredients in a clean jam jar with a tight-fitting lid and shake about to mix well. The dressing will keep for a while in the fridge.

Fruit Puddings
and Savouries

It has to be faced that puddings and diets don't lie together very comfortably. You have two choices: either adapt the rest of your eating a little to allow yourself enough pudding treats, or think 'fruit' instead of 'pudding'. It is sweet and 'changes the taste' – an expression used by my friend, Basil, to explain why it is necessary for him to eat dessert.

Partly because I am not a good pudding cook, but also because I cannot in all conscience put a recipe for treacle tart, my favourite, in a book of recipes for slimmers, I have restricted this section to fruit puddings; I have also included two savouries, which could equally well be had for a first course or snack lunch, but are often popular instead of pudding.

Official Budget Day duties included kissing for photographers on the steps of Number Eleven, en route to the House of Commons for the presentation of the Budget

Yellow Melon with Raspberries

T he flavours of melon and raspberries combine delightfully and this simple pudding also looks lush and lovely.

SERVES 8

1 lb (450g) raspberries	First make the sauce: put 5 oz (150g) of the raspberries in a saucepan with the water and the liqueur or cordial. Reserve the rest of the raspberries.
1 tablespoon water	
3 tablespoons crème de mûres if available – or use crème de cassis or	Bring to simmering point and cook gently for 8 minutes, stirring to break down the fruit.

'light' blackcurrant cordial	Take off the heat and when cool enough, process until smooth and a bit frothy. Press through a nylon sieve to remove the pips. Pour into a bowl and leave to cool, covered, until needed.
2 ripe melons of different types, Galia, Charentais or Canteloup	Cut each melon in half lengthways and scoop out the seeds. Cut each half of the biggest melon lengthways again into 4 to make 8 canoe shapes. Cut off the peel and put one 'canoe' on each plate. Slice through, into pieces, to make them easier to eat, trying to keep them in shape. Chop the flesh of the second melon into spoon-sized chunks or use a melon baller.
the reserved raspberries	Divide the melon chunks or balls and the reserved raspberries between the 8 plates. Distribute the sauce evenly between the portions, either on the melon 'canoes' or on the side, whichever you think looks prettiest. The sauce should be sweet enough to make sugar unnecessary.
a little grated fresh ginger (optional) and/or pepper	Sprinkle over a little ginger, if you like. And I like pepper over my melon.

Blueberry Pudding

This is Summer Pudding with a difference and makes use of diet products to reduce its sinfulness. It needs to be prepared the night before.

SERVES 4–6

8–9 slices of one-day-old, medium-sliced white and grainy bread, crusts removed	Line a standard 1½ pint (850ml) pudding basin with the bread, reviving your geometrical skills to ensure that there are no gaps. Keep aside a slice for the top.
1 lb 2 oz (500g) frozen 'raspberry and blueberry medley' (available from most supermarkets) 4 tablespoons 'light' cranberry juice 1 tablespoon crème de mûres, crème de cassis or 'light' blackcurrant cordial	Heat the fruit, juice and liqueur or cordial gently in a saucepan until the fruit is softened but not squashed. Using a slotted spoon, three-quarters fill the lined basin with most of the fruit and about half of the juice. Reserve the remaining juice and any fruit. Cover with the last slice of bread, fold over the edges, latch down with a saucer or plate small enough to fit inside the basin and weight with a heavy tin of baked beans or equivalent. Refrigerate overnight.
4½ oz (125g) blueberries the reserved juice and fruit 1 dessertspoon Slite	To make the coulis, cook half the blueberries and the reserved juice and fruit for a few minutes with the Slite. Liquidise into a sauce and then sieve to remove the pips. When ready to serve, run a palette knife very carefully around the inside of the basin and loosen the pudding from the sides. Place the serving dish on top and invert quickly to turn out the pudding. Pour over the coulis and surround the pudding with the

uncooked blueberries, sprinkled with more Slite, if
required.

half-fat crème fraîche or low-fat yoghurt	Serve with half-fat crème fraîche or low-fat yoghurt.

Elderflower Jelly

My dear friend and neighbour, Kisty (The Dowager Lady Hesketh, as she avoids being called) was châtelaine of what is arguably one of the most beautiful houses in England – Easton Neston at Towcester. Northamptonshire's hedges are abundant with elderflowers in June. Kisty's elderflower cordial is the best I've ever sampled and, apart from being a delicious drink, can be used to make this wonderful jelly.

When picking elderflower heads, do so in the sunshine. Not only does this make it an even more pleasurable activity than it is to start with, but also the fragrance and flavour of elderflowers picked in the sun are better. It is true! Commercial elderflower cordial is very good indeed, if expensive. It is not a sin to use that instead of making your own.

This pudding looks stunning, a shimmering jewel (see photograph). Serve on a dark plate – green or navy blue – and watch it pick up the light as it trembles. Prepare it 8 hours ahead.

SERVES 4

about 4 fl oz (120ml) elderflower cordial 14 fl oz (400ml) water	Make up the cordial with the water. Put about a fifth of the diluted cordial in a saucepan and bring to the boil. Cool for a minute.

1 sachet of powdered gelatine	Sprinkle gelatine over the hot liquid and stir briskly until completely dissolved.
	Add the rest of the diluted cordial and strain through a sieve or jelly bag to ensure the jelly will be completely translucent.
	Pour into a 1 pint (600ml) jelly mould or individual moulds. Refrigerate until set.
elderflower heads, if available, to decorate or a few Cape gooseberries (physalis), optional	When nearly ready to serve, dip the mould (or moulds) briefly into very hot water, put a serving dish on top, invert quickly, shake gently, and the jelly will plop out. Refrigerate again until ready to serve.
	If available, decorate with elderflower heads. Or Cape gooseberries go well – open their papery leaves and put them around the jelly.

Tom's Yoghurt Ice Cream

My friend Samuel, who likes puddings very much more than vegetables but who nevertheless succeeded in losing a great deal of weight recently – he says thanks to a specially-modified version of this diet – gave me a sorbetière for my birthday. Not the huge one that costs a fortune and needs a new kitchen to house, but the type that has to be put in the freezer well beforehand and then churns as the mixture freezes. It saves a lot of bother. I am told that it is perfectly possible to make excellent sorbets and ice creams without a machine – but all I know is that you are required to stay at home because you have to return to the ice to beat up the crystals during the freezing process.

It was my grown-up son, Tom, who got the job of understanding the instructions and mechanism of the machine. Now he has it off pat. He rather likes cooking anyway, ever since the last year at his (all boys) school where the optional cookery course was the most over-subscribed of the whole sixth form curriculum. Poor Tom didn't get in.

His strawberry ice cream, made with yoghurt, is the best I've ever had. You could equally well make it with other fruit – blackcurrants are particularly good.

First chill all your equipment.

SERVES 4–6

1 lb (450g) strawberries 1 oz (25g) Slite 10 oz (275g) yoghurt	Hull 12 oz (350g) of the strawberries and reserve the rest. Put the hulled strawberries in a processor and whizz to break them up. Add the Slite and yoghurt to the processor and blend until well mixed and smooth. Chill the mixture for at least an hour in the fridge, then churn in the machine until it looks like ice cream, and is beginning to stick to the sides. My machine starts to dance in a peculiar way when this point is reached. Put it into a rigid freezerproof container, cover and freeze until ready to use.
the reserved strawberries *Fruit Coulis* (see recipe on page 149), optional	30–45 minutes before serving, transfer the ice cream from the freezer to the fridge to give it a chance to soften a little. Hull and slice the remaining strawberries and serve them with the ice cream, which looks nicest divided into portions with a round scoop. If you like, pour some previously made *Fruit Coulis* over each portion.

Kiwi Citrus Sorbet

This sorbet makes a tangy and refreshing change of taste, not least because of the inclusion of Curaçao Triple Sec, a flavour introduced to Tom and then the household by my beloved step-daughter, Horatia, who lives in New York.

Chill all the equipment you are going to use before starting this recipe.

SERVES 4–6

1 orange	Using a potato peeler, remove the zest from the orange and limes and reserve.
2 limes	
4 kiwi fruits	Cut the orange and the limes in half and extract the juice from them.
4 fl oz (120ml) orange juice	Cut the kiwi fruits in half and scoop out all the flesh and juice with a teaspoon.
	Put in the processor with the orange and lime juice and blend until smooth. Set aside.

³/₄ pint (450ml) water	Heat the water to boiling point with the Slite and zests.
2 oz (50g) Slite	Stir constantly over a medium heat until the sugar has dissolved.
the reserved orange and lime zests	
	Add the alcohol and simmer for 5 minutes.
1¹/₂ fl oz (40ml) Curaçao Triple Sec or Grand Marnier	Remove from the heat, add the gelatine and stir briskly until completely dissolved. If you have trouble with the gelatine, stand it in a warm place, stirring intermittently until there are no lumps.
¹/₂ sachet of powdered gelatine	Sieve the liquid.
	Add to it the kiwi flesh and citrus juices. (You can leave in the black kiwi pips if you like to add crunch.)
	Stir, cool and refrigerate for at least an hour.
	Put the cold mixture into the ice cream maker and churn until ice crystals form.

1 egg white	Beat the egg white with a fork.
	Add to the machine once the mixture is beginning to thicken.
	When everything is well amalgamated and looks the right consistency, turn into a rigid freezerproof container, cover and freeze until ready to serve. The consistency is volatile so don't dawdle at this point.

| 1 extra kiwi fruit
a few sprigs of mint | Decorate each serving with slices of kiwi fruit and/or mint. |

Purple Hearts

For this recipe, you will need a round sieve, a bowl it will sit on, muslin to line the sieve or a jelly bag. Use heart-shaped moulds with a removable base, if possible (available in some supermarkets), base-lined with non-stick baking paper. You need to prepare the pudding 8 hours in advance, to leave overnight if you are an owl or all day if a lark.

It is essential to drain the quark (a very low-fat cheese) and yoghurt mixture. Do not be tempted to skip this boring stage or the pudding will not set properly and will have an unpleasant yellow pool around it when turned out. If you own porcelain cœur à la crème moulds with perforations in the bottom, you can drain the mixture in them, of course.

These *Purple Hearts* are a lot less fattening than the classic ones à la crème (see photograph). This recipe contains uncooked egg white.

SERVES 6

9 oz (250g) very low-fat quark	Line a round sieve with muslin or a jelly bag, and stand it over a bowl.
a 5 oz (150g) tub low-fat yoghurt	Place the quark, yoghurt, Slite and cassis or cordial in another bowl and mix together with a fork. Scoop the mixture into the sieve.
about 3 teaspoons Slite to taste	Leave in the fridge for about two hours or as long as it takes for the whey to drip out.
2–3 tablespoons crème de cassis or 'light' blackcurrant cordial	

2 egg whites	Line 6 moulds with non-stick baking paper.
	In a clean, dry large bowl (preferably copper), whisk the egg whites into soft peaks.
	Fold into the drained pudding mixture, quickly but thoroughly. Divide the mixture between the moulds.
	Refrigerate for several hours or overnight.

4 oz (110g) blackcurrants (use blackberries or blueberries if blackcurrants are not available)	To make the coulis, reserve a few pieces of fruit for decoration, then place the rest with the Slite, and the cassis or cordial, in a heavy-based saucepan. Bring to simmering point over a medium heat, then cook gently for 10 minutes.
1 dessertspoon Slite	Process until smooth and pass through a sieve.
3 tablespoons crème de cassis or 'light' blackcurrant cordial	To serve, turn the hearts out of the moulds onto white or glass individual plates. Spoon the coulis around the edge of each heart or use a piping bag, if you are that sort.

the reserved fruit	Decorate each serving with the reserved fruit and lemon balm.
6 small lemon balm sprigs	

Nectarines in Honey Sauce

T his pudding looks and tastes gorgeous and is simplicity itself. Part of its appeal is that the fruit is presented fully prepared, and the only effort required is to put it in your mouth. I've always thought fruit prepared for you is one of life's luxuries, to be indulged in on holiday.

SERVES 4

4 perfect, ripe nectarines	Peel the nectarines (a doddle if using the method described for oranges on page 35). Carefully cut each fruit in half and extract the stone.
2 dessertspoons runny honey (lime blossom, if at all possible) the juice of 1 lime $^1/_2$ teaspoon very finely chopped zest of lime	Warm the honey, lime juice and zest gently in a saucepan. When ready to serve, pour the warm sauce into the 'bowls' of each nectarine half.

Rainbow Jelly

There may be seven colours in a rainbow but this four-colour jelly looks most attractive, especially in stemmed champagne flutes or wine glasses. Children love it. It is very easy indeed to do but you do need to remember to start it 24 hours in advance of serving as you have to let each jelly set before adding the next.

You can make any number of delicious jellies for puddings with naturally sweet fruit juices – mandarin juice jelly with tinned mandarin segments in it is particularly popular in our house, so is blueberry and cranberry juice jelly. But beware: some fruits will not cooperate in jelly-making – kiwi and pineapple are two. You could also splash out on a wine jelly using a good, sweet pudding wine.

The quantities given make 8 glasses of jelly, assuming each glass takes ¼ pint (150ml).

SERVES 8

½ pint each (300ml) of 4 different fruit juices, chosen for colour, flavour and lack of added sugar. You can certainly use the freshly squeezed varieties but don't then expect the jelly to be translucent – you might prefer to strain off the 'bits' or use 'smooth' juice

2 sachets of powdered gelatine

First decide on your colour scheme. It is a good idea to start with orange at the bottom because it tends to be the most solid-looking, followed by either apple and elderflower, lemon or lime (translucent), then a raspberry-based juice and finally blackcurrant.

To make the first jelly, heat half of the first juice to boiling point, let it cool a little and then briskly stir in half a sachet of gelatine.

Leave to stand in a warm place until the gelatine is completely dissolved. If in any doubt, strain through a jelly bag.

Add the rest of the half-pint of juice and when absolutely cold, pour equal quantities into each of 8 wine glasses. Put in the fridge.

When the first jelly is firmly set, make the second jelly in
    exactly the same way.
When it is cool, pour it into each glass on top of the first
    jelly.
Refrigerate to set.
Repeat the process for the third and fourth jellies.
Leave to set firmly and that is it.

Fruit Coulis

All 'coulis' means is puréed sauce, usually of fruit or vegetables. A well-flavoured, rich sauce poured over choice fresh fruits makes the simplest but most delicious of puddings.

The trouble with the traditional method of making coulis is that a lot of icing sugar is used. You can avoid this by cooking the fruit in an appropriate liqueur and so long as you boil off the alcohol, you are thereby reducing its most fattening element. Also, you don't need to use a great deal of liqueur to impart a strong flavour. Double whammy for calories.

You can adapt this recipe to more or less any kind of robust fruit (I'd not bother with watermelon, for instance) but the combination I find most useful, and which emerges a spectacular colour, is of raspberries and either blackcurrants or blueberries.

MAKES 8 FL OZ (225ML)

4¹/₂ oz (125g) raspberries
4¹/₂ oz (125g) fresh or
   frozen blackcurrants
   or blueberries
	Pick over the fruits and rinse briefly.

3 fl oz (75ml) crème de mûres or crème de cassis	Put all the ingredients in a heavy-based saucepan over a medium heat. Bring to the boil and simmer for 5 minutes.
2 fl oz (55ml) water	Then, as soon as the fruits are visibly softening, turn into a processor and blend to as smooth a consistency as possible. If you mind about pips, press the coulis through a sieve.
1 dessertspoon Slite	Chill, covered, until ready to serve.

Quirky-Quarky Soufflés

There is no doubt that a cooking reputation is improved by the production of soufflés, yet people are often scared stiff of trying them. Really the most difficult part of the process is when serving, since a soufflé will deflate rapidly in cold air – just ensure that the eaters don't dilly-dally at the crucial moment. It is also essential to complete quickly and effectively the process of beating and incorporating the egg whites. Otherwise, think of a soufflé as just a cheese sauce with fluffy egg whites added: not remotely intimidating.

As the main ingredient in this recipe is quark, a low-fat soft cheese, it is considerably less fattening than an orthodox soufflé.

Have all the ingredients at room temperature.

MAKES 10–12 INDIVIDUAL SOUFFLÉS

5 large eggs	Preheat the oven to 180°C (350°F, Gas 4, Aga baking oven) and make sure that the shelf is so positioned that the soufflés have plenty of room to rise.
	Separate the eggs very carefully. It doesn't matter if the yolks have a bit of white in them but the whites must be completely yolk-free. Set aside in separate bowls.

1½ oz (40g) unsalted butter	Use some of the butter to smear the insides of 10 or 12 ramekins. Be sure to grease the lips of the dishes so the soufflés can slide up and beyond the top.
about 1 tablespoon grated Parmesan cheese	Sprinkle Parmesan around the inside of each dish.
1 tablespoon plain flour	Put the rest of the butter in a heavy-based saucepan and melt over a medium heat, then add the flour and mix with a wooden spoon. Add the milk and water, a little at a time, stirring continuously to make a smooth white sauce. (Send to the blender or whisk if there are any lumps: it is important for the base sauce to be completely smooth.)
8 fl oz (225ml) semi-skimmed milk	
2 fl oz (55ml) water	

1 oz (25g) Stilton or other strong cheese, to taste	Crumble the Stilton into the sauce and cook until melted.
	Lower the heat and stir in the quark, mustard, if using, and salt and pepper. Stir until smooth.
9 oz (250g) virtually fat-free quark	Beat the egg yolks and, off the heat, add them to the sauce. Transfer to a large bowl and stand in a warm place until required.
1 teaspoon mustard powder (optional)	Prepare a *bain-marie*: using a baking tin large enough to take all the ramekins, put them in and add hot water to the tin until it comes half way up the sides of the ramekins.
salt and pepper	
4 of the reserved egg yolks	

the reserved egg whites	Whisk the egg whites with a pinch of salt until stiff. A copper bowl helps enormously and so does a hand-held electric whisk. Move the bowl around, rather than the whisk, to maximise the air beaten in.
	Stir a tablespoon of egg white into the cheesy sauce and then, very quickly but thoroughly, fold in the rest of the whites. A metal spoon is usually recommended for this purpose, but a rubber spatula is very good too and I find it easier.
	Immediately divide the mixture between the ramekins in the *bain-marie* and then place quickly into the preheated

oven for 15 minutes. It is wonderful if your oven has a glass door as you can see your soufflés growing. If it hasn't, do not be tempted to open the oven to peep or your soufflés might deflate.

Take out, allow to cool, cover with clingwrap and refrigerate until required. Or, if you want to have them straightaway, continue to cook for another 5 minutes or so until puffy and browned.

When ready to serve the soufflés, preheat the oven as before, place the ramekins on a baking tray (there is no need for a *bain-marie*) and bake for 10-15 minutes. They rise again miraculously, bubbling and browned (see photograph).

Goats' Cheese on a Wholemeal Muffin with Truffle (v)

Occasionally, one really wants cheese on toast. Make it a special, rare treat, and have a jar of the necessary topping in the kitchen, ready for the day – it keeps for months. This recipe makes a smart savoury for a dinner party.

The truffle oil is very expensive – and you must buy the best – but it can be re-used to add a fabulous flavour to mushroom, rice and pasta dishes. As for the real truffle, well, that is a serious luxury: add it if you possibly can.

You will need a large, pristinely clean jam jar with a lid.

SERVES 8

8 rounds of goats' cheese, weighing about 1 oz (25g) each a small, ripe black Périgord truffle (optional) enough truffle oil to cover: up to ½ pint (300ml)	Put the rounds of cheese into the jar. As you put each piece in, shave over a sliver of truffle, if using. (A potato peeler will do for the job.) Now cover with the oil, ensuring that every bit of cheese is covered. Seal the jar tightly and store to allow the flavours to steep for a few days.

---

4 wholemeal muffins 8 rounds of prepared goats' cheese in truffle oil pepper	When you decide to serve this savoury, preheat the grill. Split each muffin in half. Toast lightly on their outsides. Arrange on a grill pan. Put a round of cheese, carefully picked out with tongs from the jar and leaving behind as much oil as possible, on each muffin half – the uncooked side. Grind pepper over. Grill until softened, bubbling and a little brown.

Index